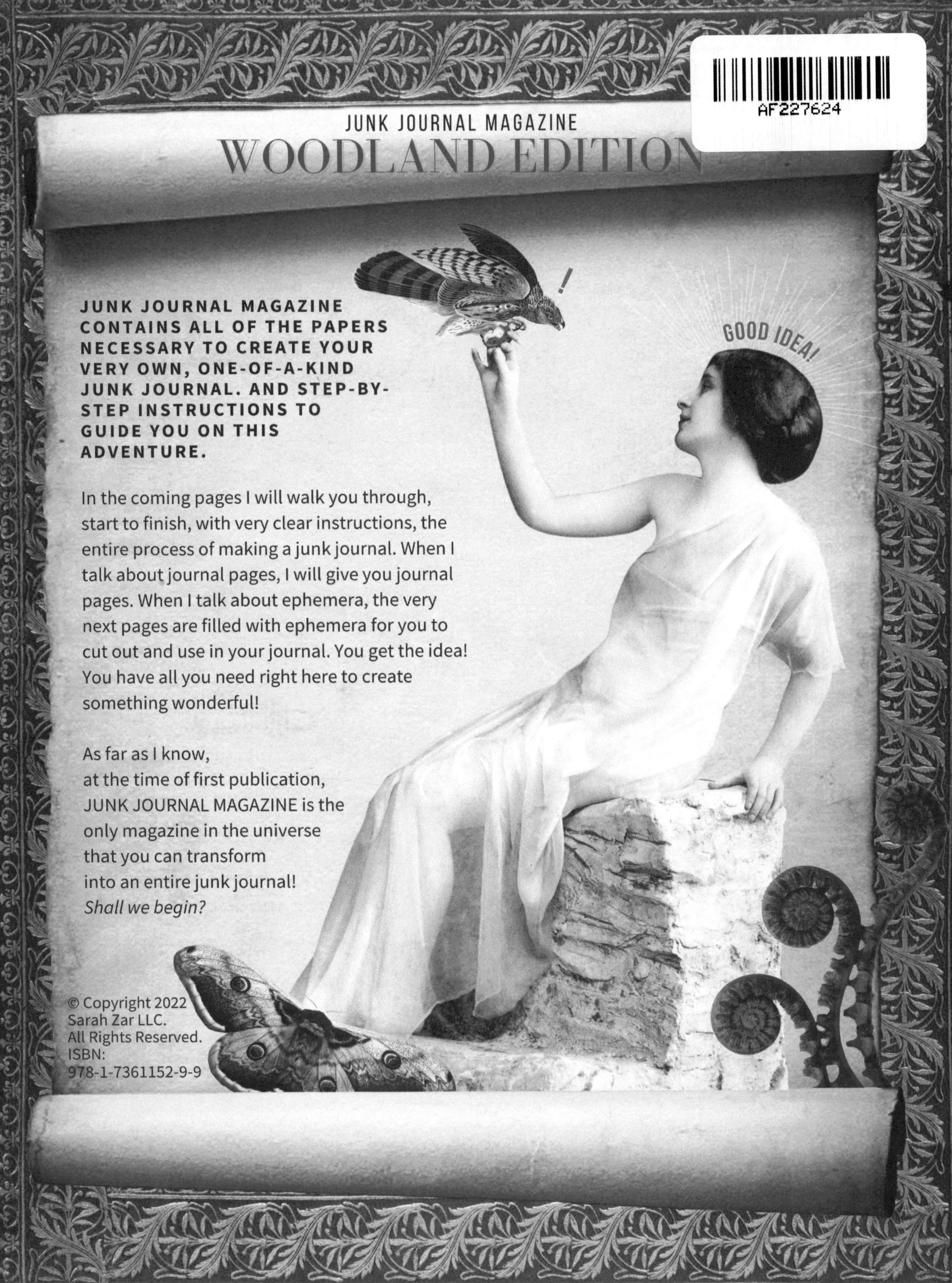

JUNK JOURNAL MAGAZINE
WOODLAND EDITION

JUNK JOURNAL MAGAZINE CONTAINS ALL OF THE PAPERS NECESSARY TO CREATE YOUR VERY OWN, ONE-OF-A-KIND JUNK JOURNAL. AND STEP-BY-STEP INSTRUCTIONS TO GUIDE YOU ON THIS ADVENTURE.

In the coming pages I will walk you through, start to finish, with very clear instructions, the entire process of making a junk journal. When I talk about journal pages, I will give you journal pages. When I talk about ephemera, the very next pages are filled with ephemera for you to cut out and use in your journal. You get the idea! You have all you need right here to create something wonderful!

As far as I know, at the time of first publication, JUNK JOURNAL MAGAZINE is the only magazine in the universe that you can transform into an entire junk journal! *Shall we begin?*

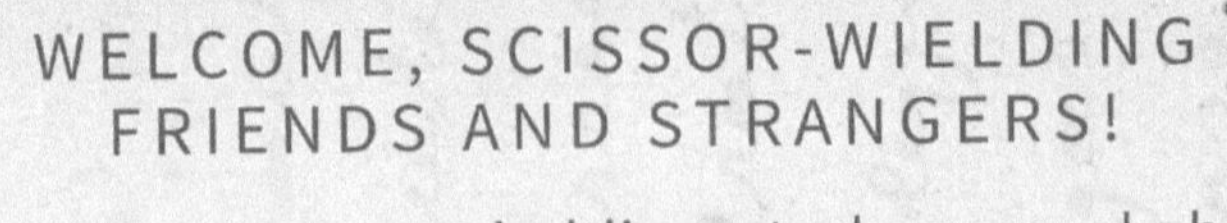

WELCOME, SCISSOR-WIELDING FRIENDS AND STRANGERS!

In your hands, you are holding a truly unusual object. *Junk Journal Magazine** guides you through the process of transforming these pages into a gorgeous journal, using everyday items you probably have at home. But not just any journal! **Your journal will be filled with beautiful papers, envelopes, bookmarks, places to record ideas and hide secret thoughts.**

One page at a time, I will show you how to take apart this magazine, and turn it into a completed work of art, called a junk journal. A junk journal is a one-of-a-kind book you can write in that is made from a wide assortment of papers or materials. Things that might otherwise be thrown away ('junk') can be combined to create a treasured book unlike anything else in all the land.

YOU TOO CAN BECOME A PAPER MAGE!
Have you ever wondered what it would feel like to wake up one day, and suddenly see the world in an entirely different way? What if every time you saw a scrap of colorful paper or ribbon, it began to dance in your mind's eye, spinning and folding, and fitting together with other scraps, coalescing into a beautiful and totally original book, unlike anything you've seen before?

I'm here to tell you that this power is within your grasp. [Glue] Stick with me, and soon you will have a unique and artful handmade journal that you can hold and marvel at, keep to write in, or give as a gift to a loved one. But you'll also have gained something much more valuable... the knowledge and ability to turn ordinary objects into stunning journals that can dazzle, delight, and inspire.

Everything around you, from a string to torn page, to an autumn leaf on the ground will suddenly be filled with potential. You will see that you are moving through a universe full of wondrous craft supplies, just waiting to be gathered!

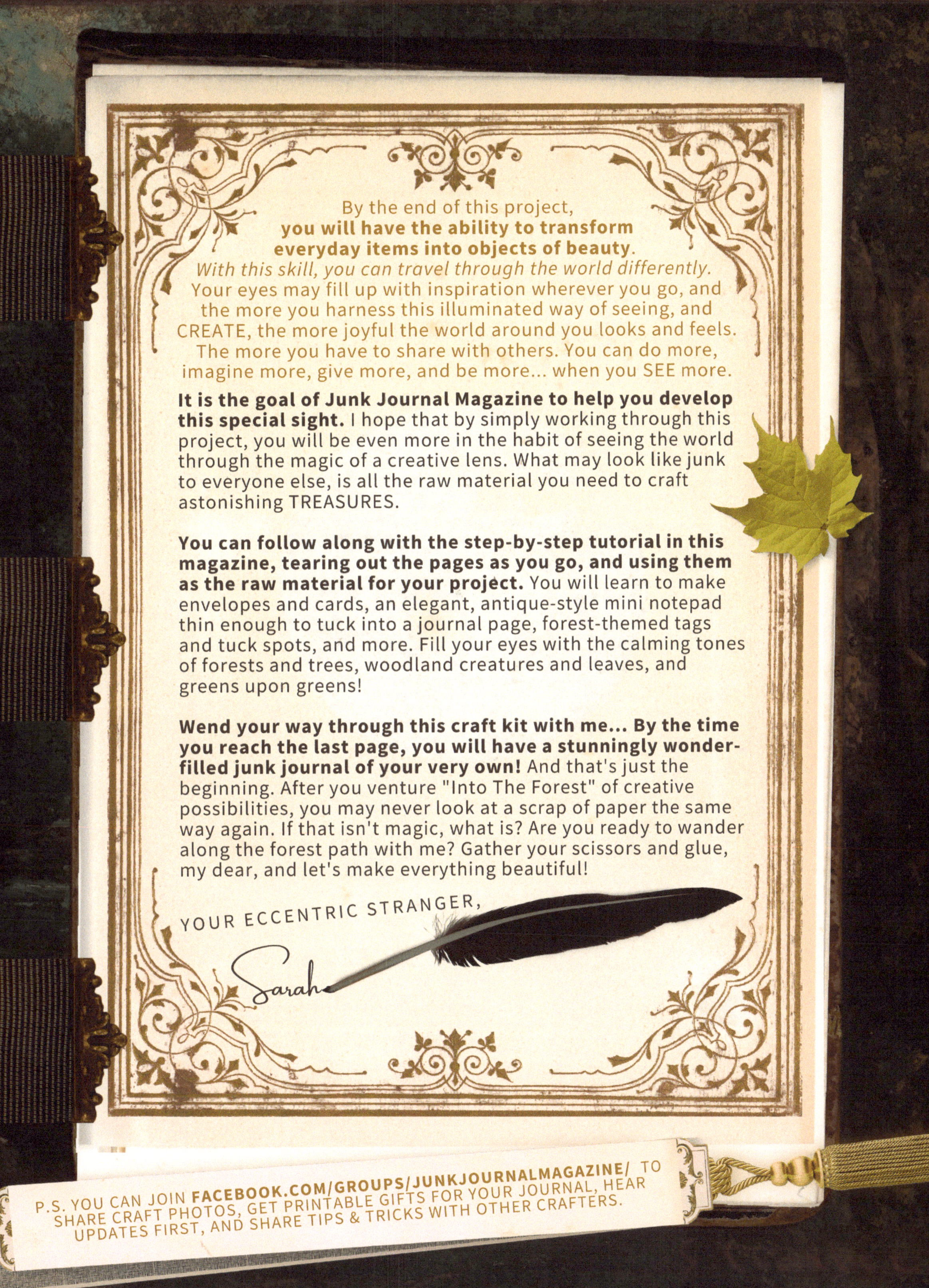

By the end of this project,
**you will have the ability to transform
everyday items into objects of beauty**.
With this skill, you can travel through the world differently.
Your eyes may fill up with inspiration wherever you go, and
the more you harness this illuminated way of seeing, and
CREATE, the more joyful the world around you looks and feels.
The more you have to share with others. You can do more,
imagine more, give more, and be more... when you SEE more.

**It is the goal of Junk Journal Magazine to help you develop
this special sight.** I hope that by simply working through this
project, you will be even more in the habit of seeing the world
through the magic of a creative lens. What may look like junk
to everyone else, is all the raw material you need to craft
astonishing TREASURES.

**You can follow along with the step-by-step tutorial in this
magazine, tearing out the pages as you go, and using them
as the raw material for your project.** You will learn to make
envelopes and cards, an elegant, antique-style mini notepad
thin enough to tuck into a journal page, forest-themed tags
and tuck spots, and more. Fill your eyes with the calming tones
of forests and trees, woodland creatures and leaves, and
greens upon greens!

**Wend your way through this craft kit with me... By the time
you reach the last page, you will have a stunningly wonder-
filled junk journal of your very own!** And that's just the
beginning. After you venture "Into The Forest" of creative
possibilities, you may never look at a scrap of paper the same
way again. If that isn't magic, what is? Are you ready to wander
along the forest path with me? Gather your scissors and glue,
my dear, and let's make everything beautiful!

YOUR ECCENTRIC STRANGER,

Sarah

INSTRUCTIONS

Follow along to transform your copy of *Junk Journal Magazine* into a one-of-a- kind JUNK JOURNAL!

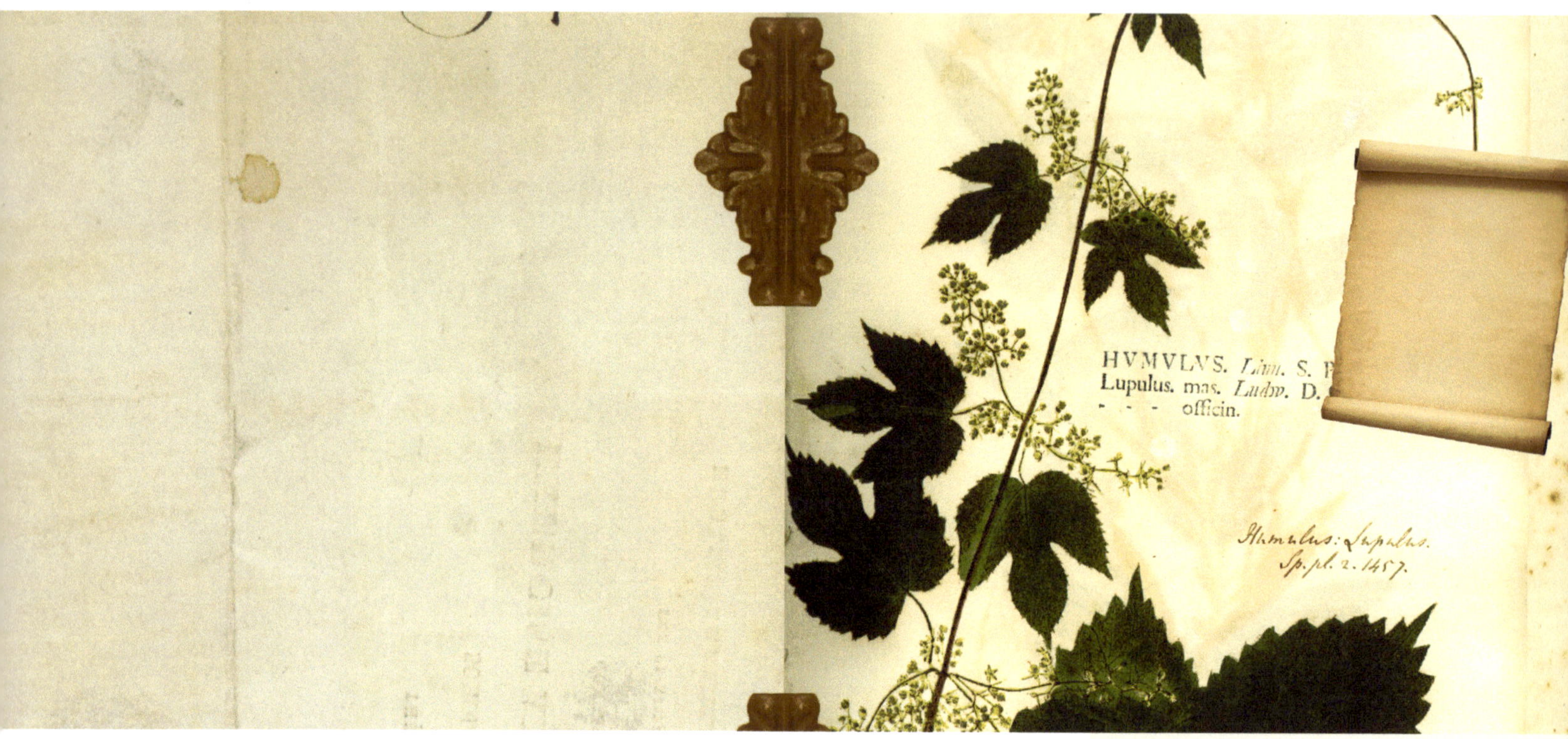

Materials List

ITEMS TO GATHER

- A cat, if you have one. This will ensure that you pay adequate attention to your ribbons. Ribbon, if you have any.
- Scissors, scalpel, and ruler
- Acid-free glue stick
- Double-sided tape
- A straight or curved sewing needle.
- Waxed bookbinding string, or any other string/embroidery floss you have.
- Cardboard/cereal box or a manila folder.
- An awl, or some other pointy object you can use to poke holes in paper.
- A piece of scrap wood or a cutting board you can dent.
- *Optional: a 'bone folder' or a spoon, a brayer or rolling pin or credit card to flatten glued papers, and a craft mat.*

How To Assemble A Junk Journal

If you've never made a junk journal before, this is a simple, yet elegant way to do it! These pages contain all the paper you need to create a woodland junk journal. I'll walk you through every step, so you won't be doing this alone. Gather your materials, and then we can begin!

Step 1

Start by using a scalpel to cut out all the pages between this one and STEP 2. I recommend using a ruler to guide the blade so you get a nice, neat line. This has the extra advantage of protecting the paper from tearing in the wrong place.

TABLE OF CONTENTS

INTO THE FOREST

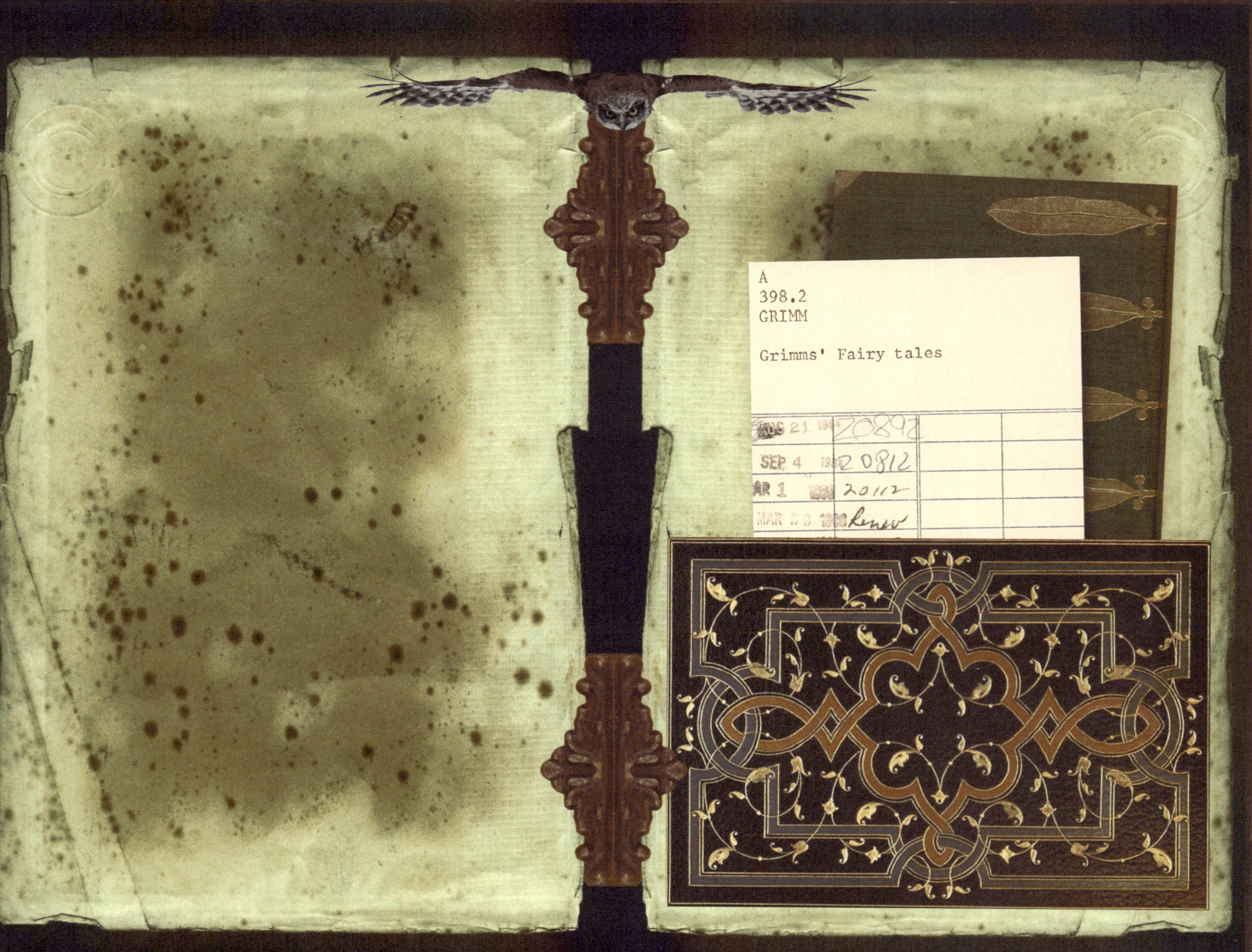
A
398.2
GRIMM
Grimms' Fairy tales
AUG 21 194
SEP 4 1992
AR 1
MAR 23
Renew

Robert Mankind & G.E. Whiting (1831.1.1831)
Jany 1. 1831

HVMVLVS. Linn. S. P.
Lupulus. mas. Ludov. D.
officin.

Humulus lupulus.
Sp. pl. 2. 1457.

79.

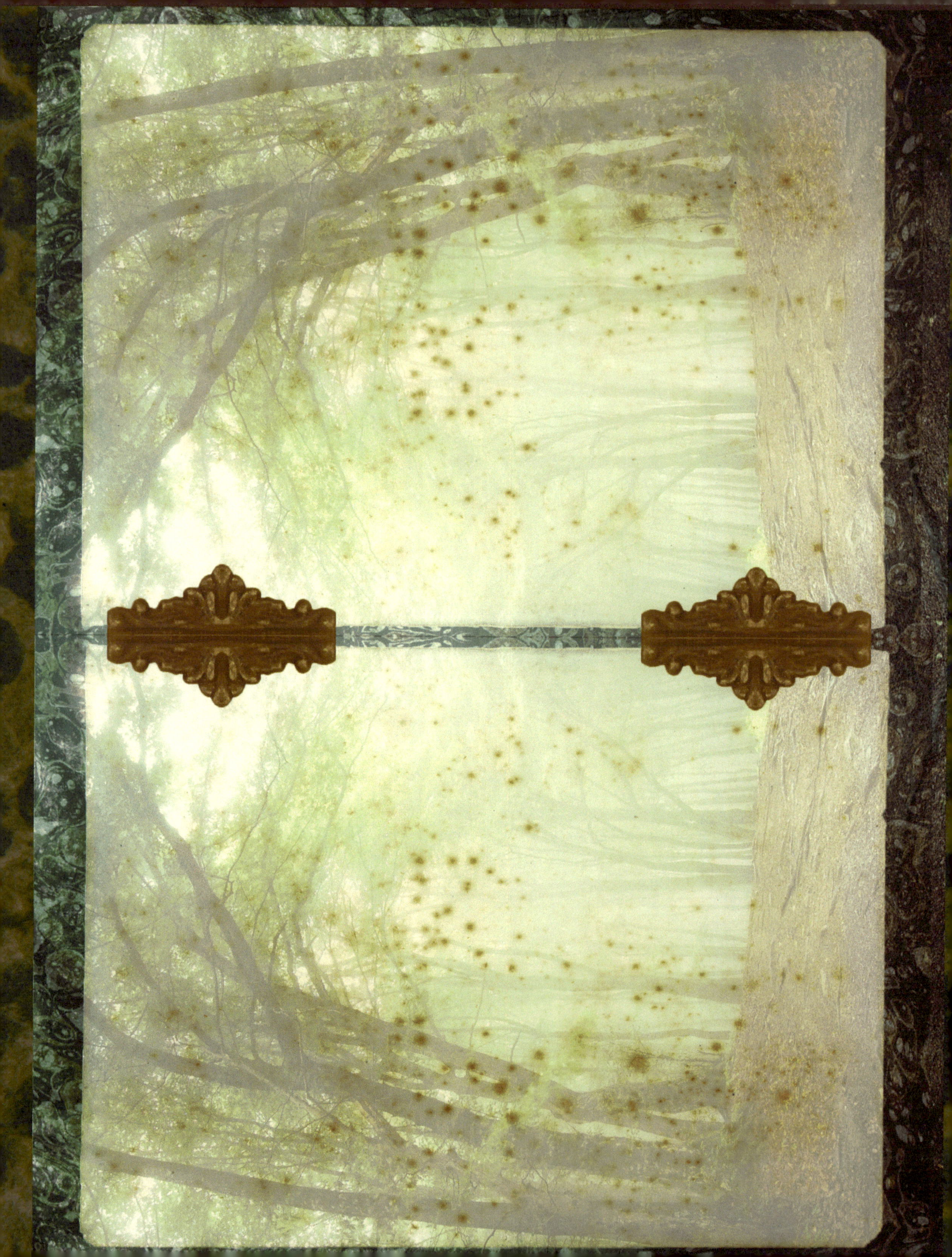

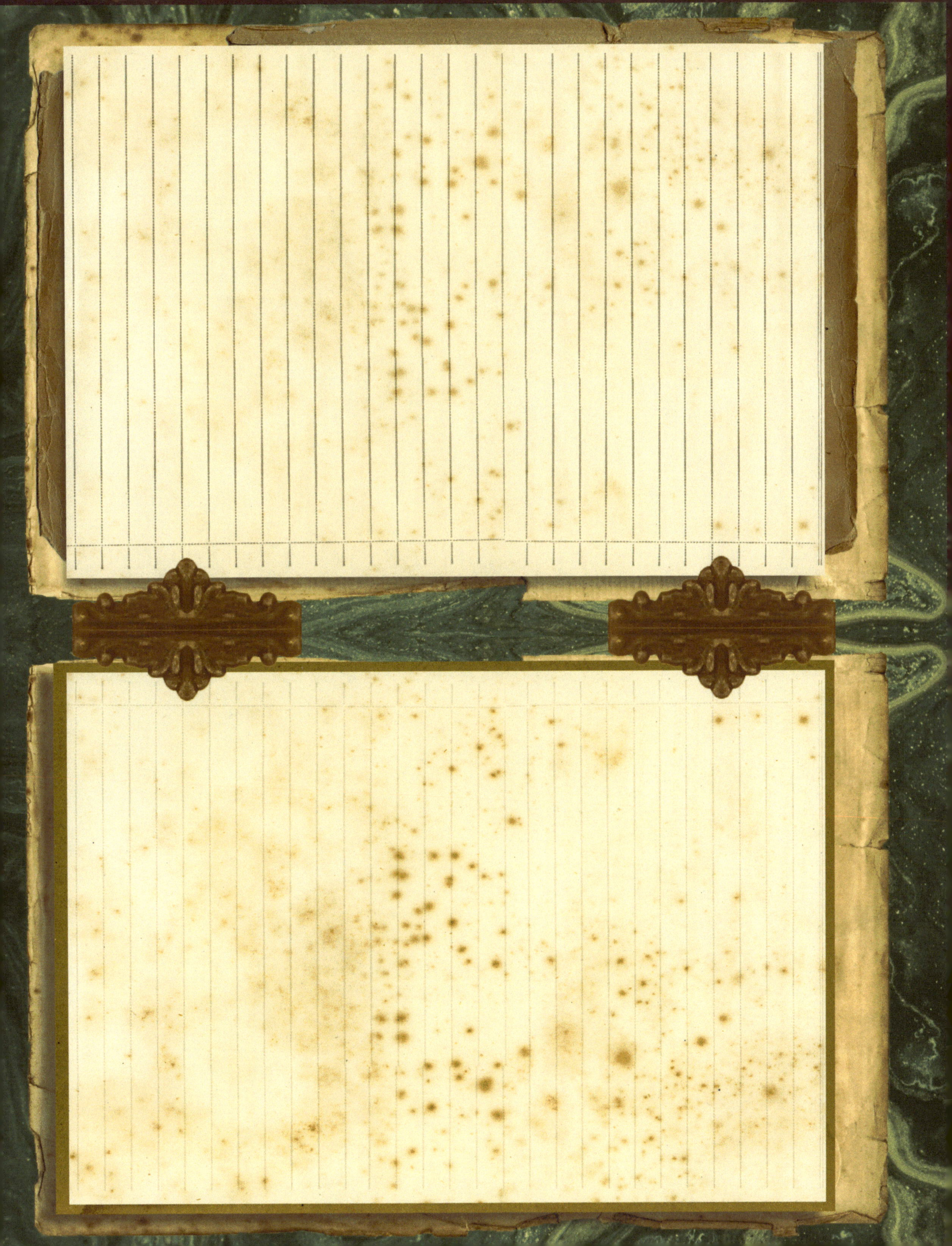

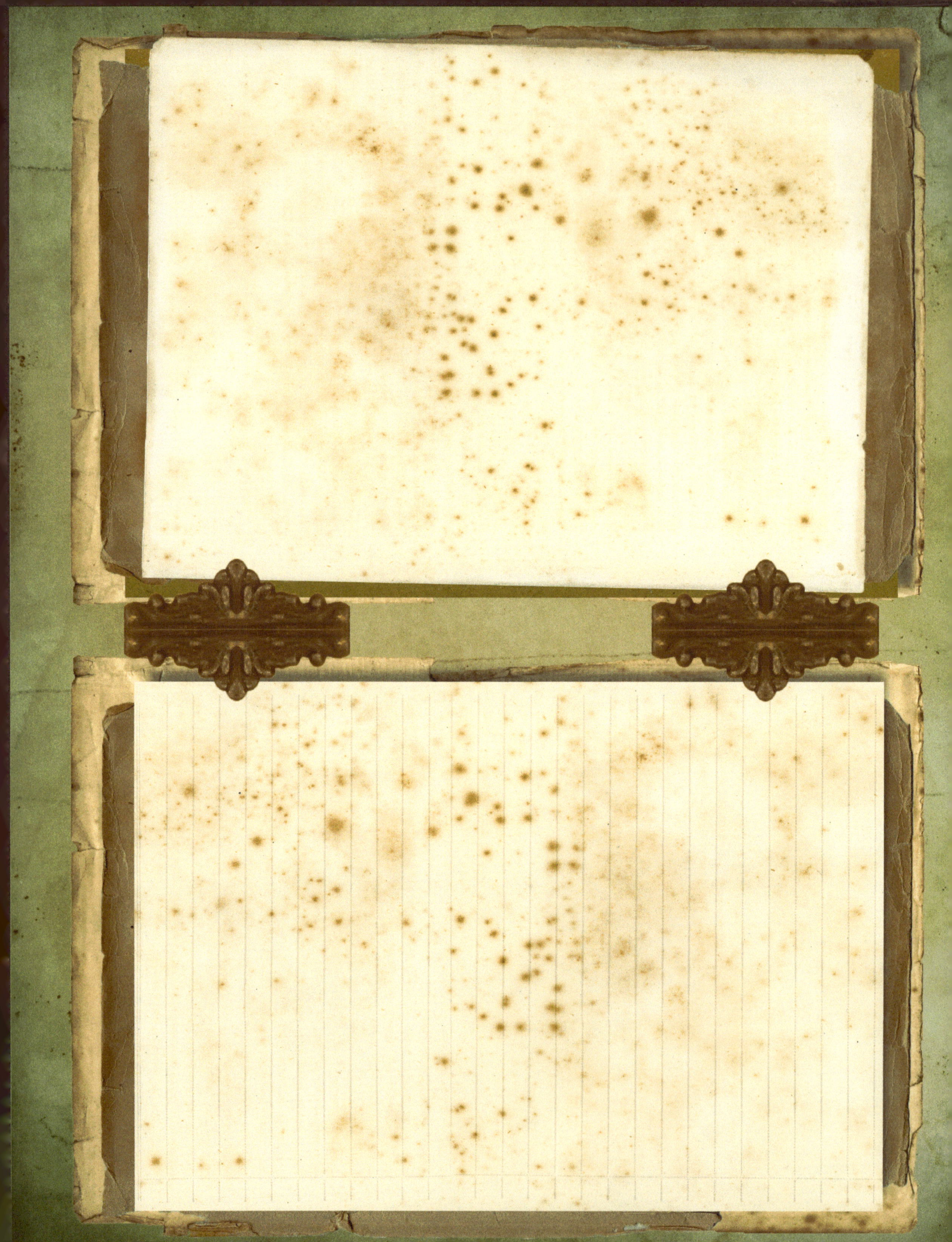

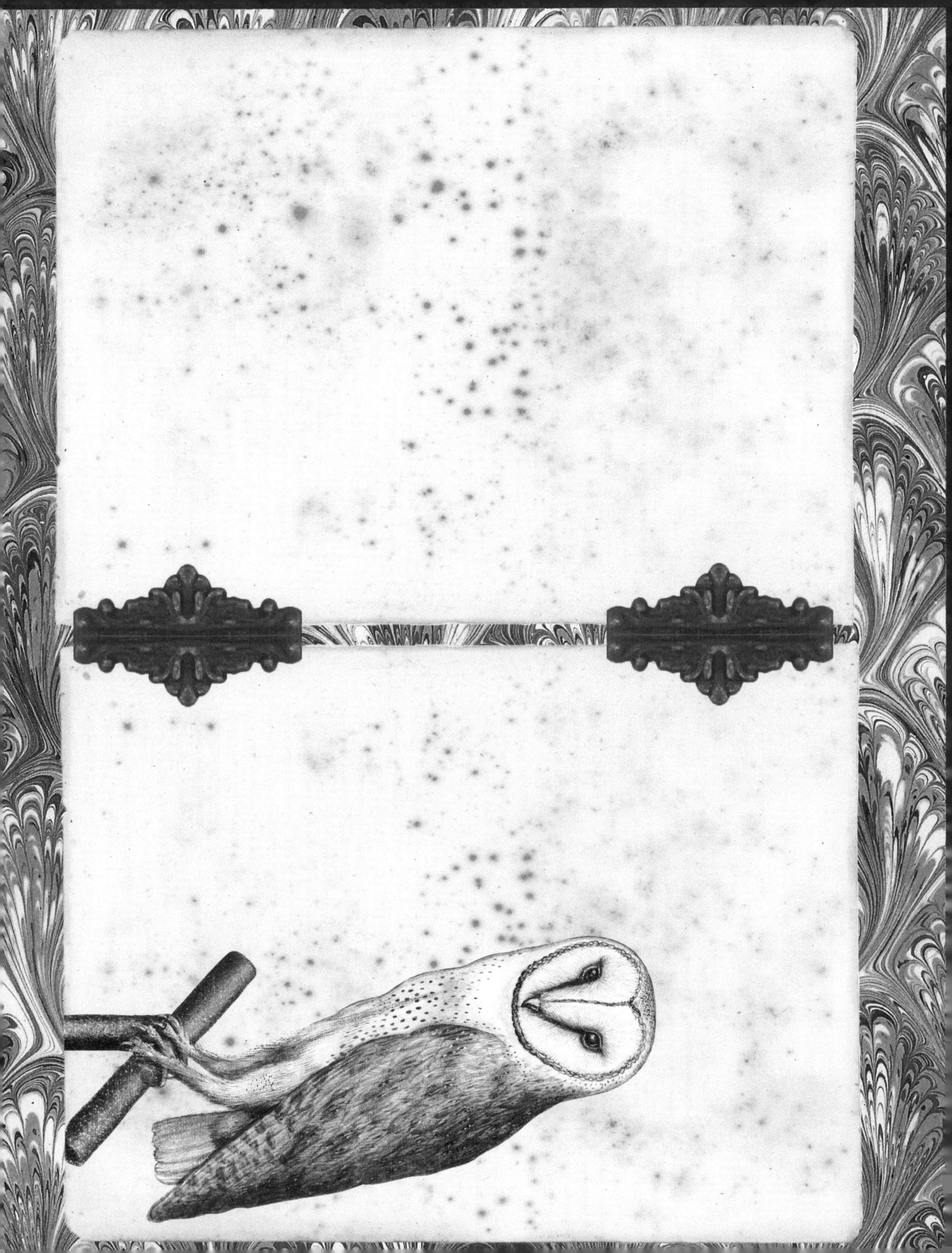

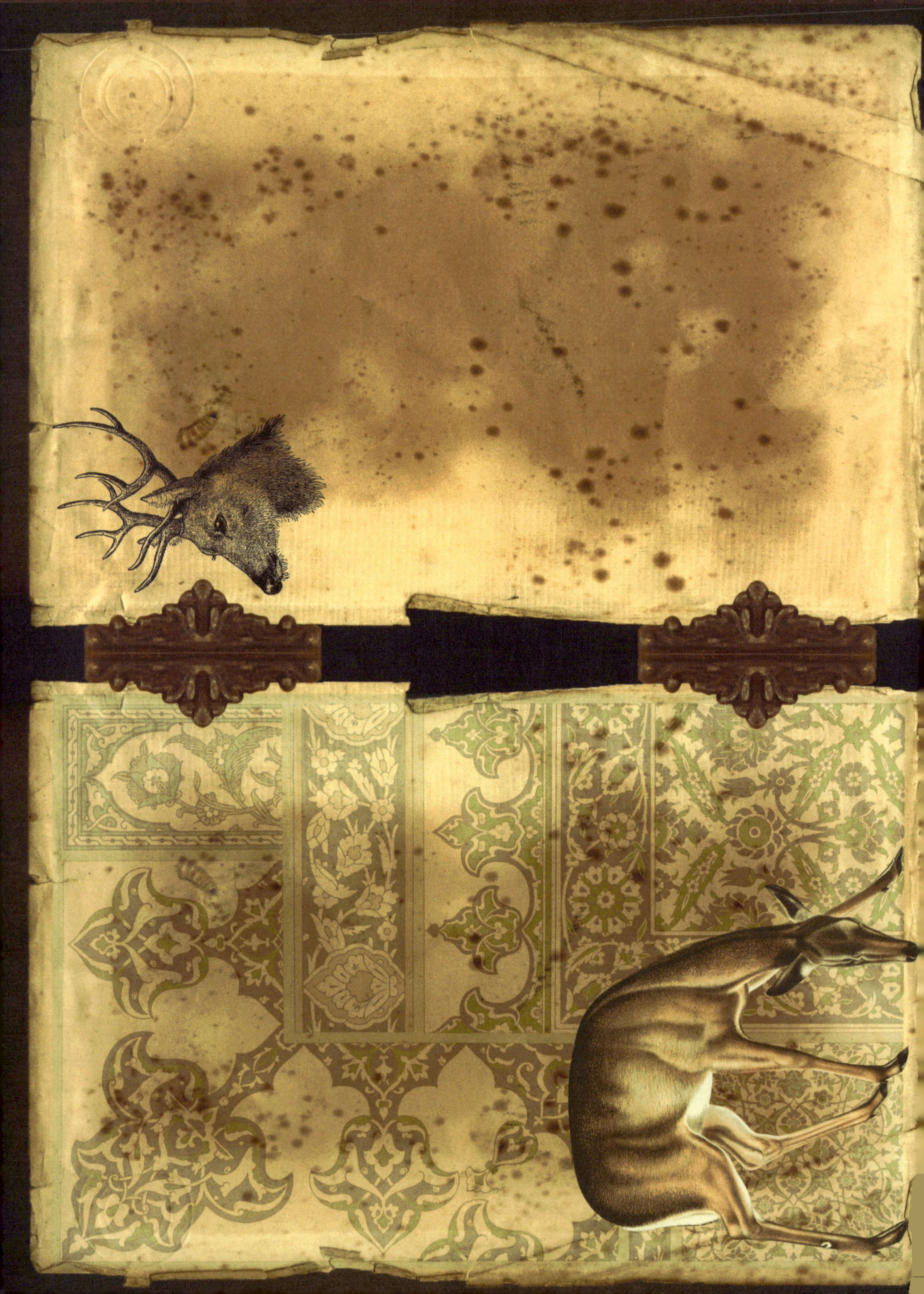

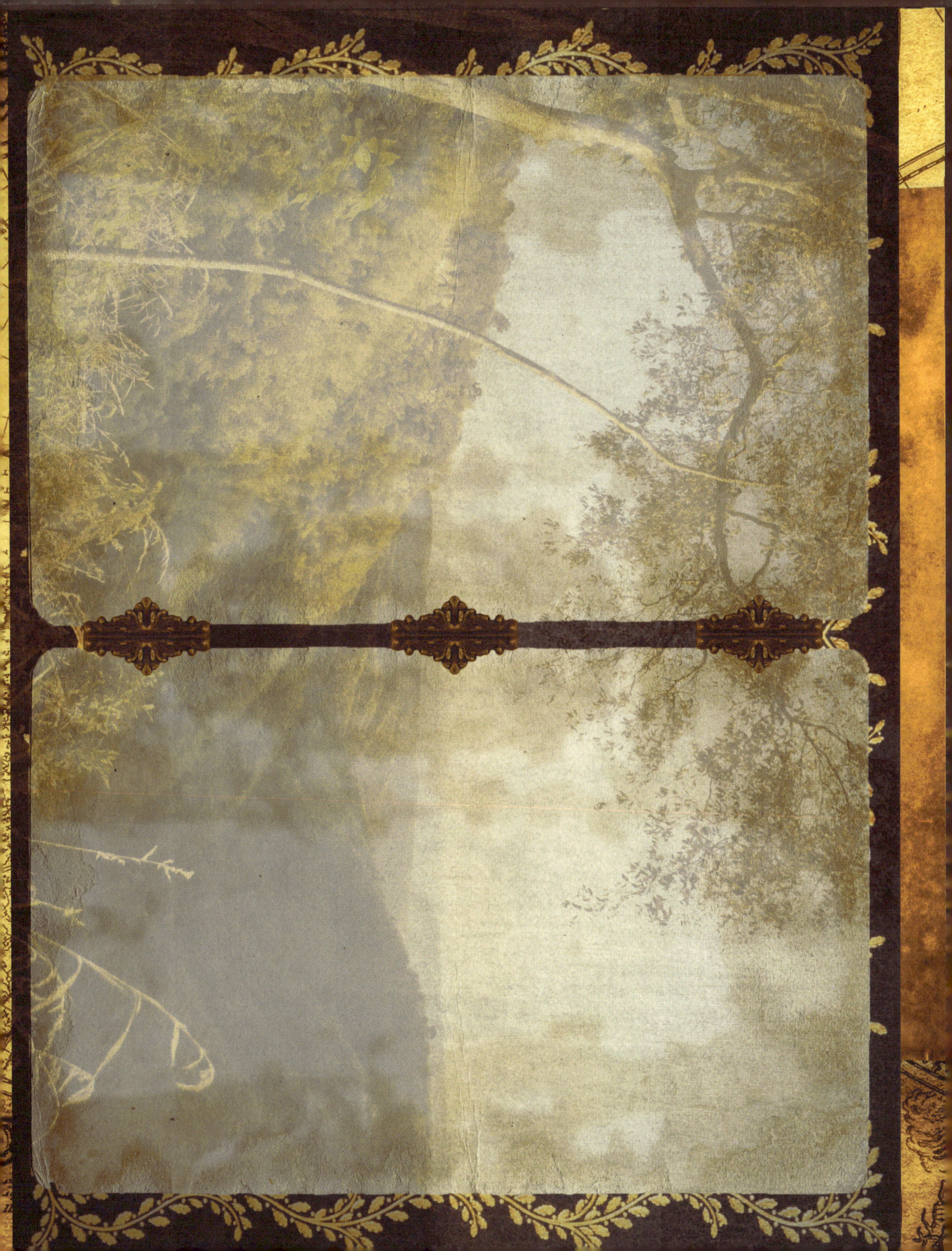

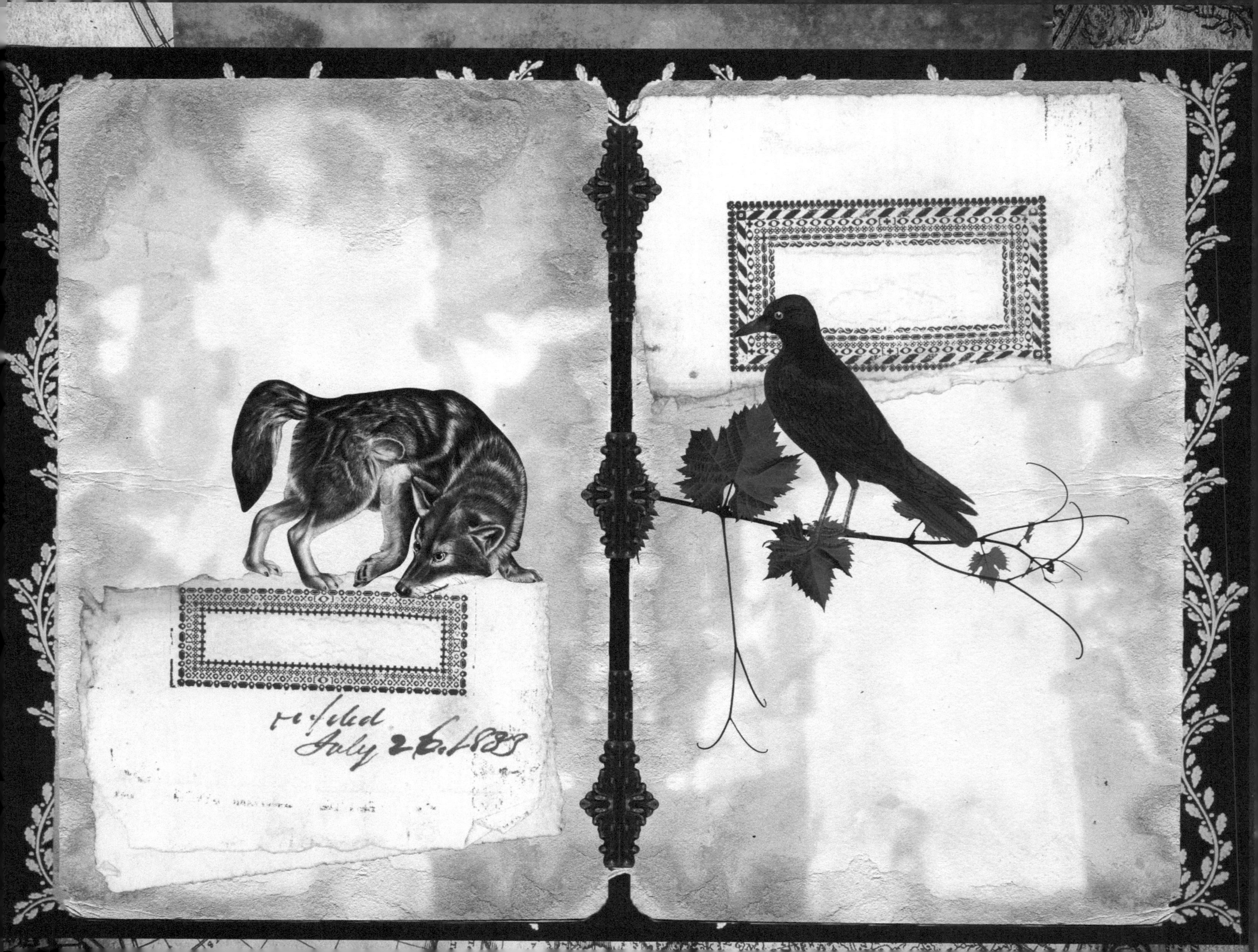
replied
July 26. 1888

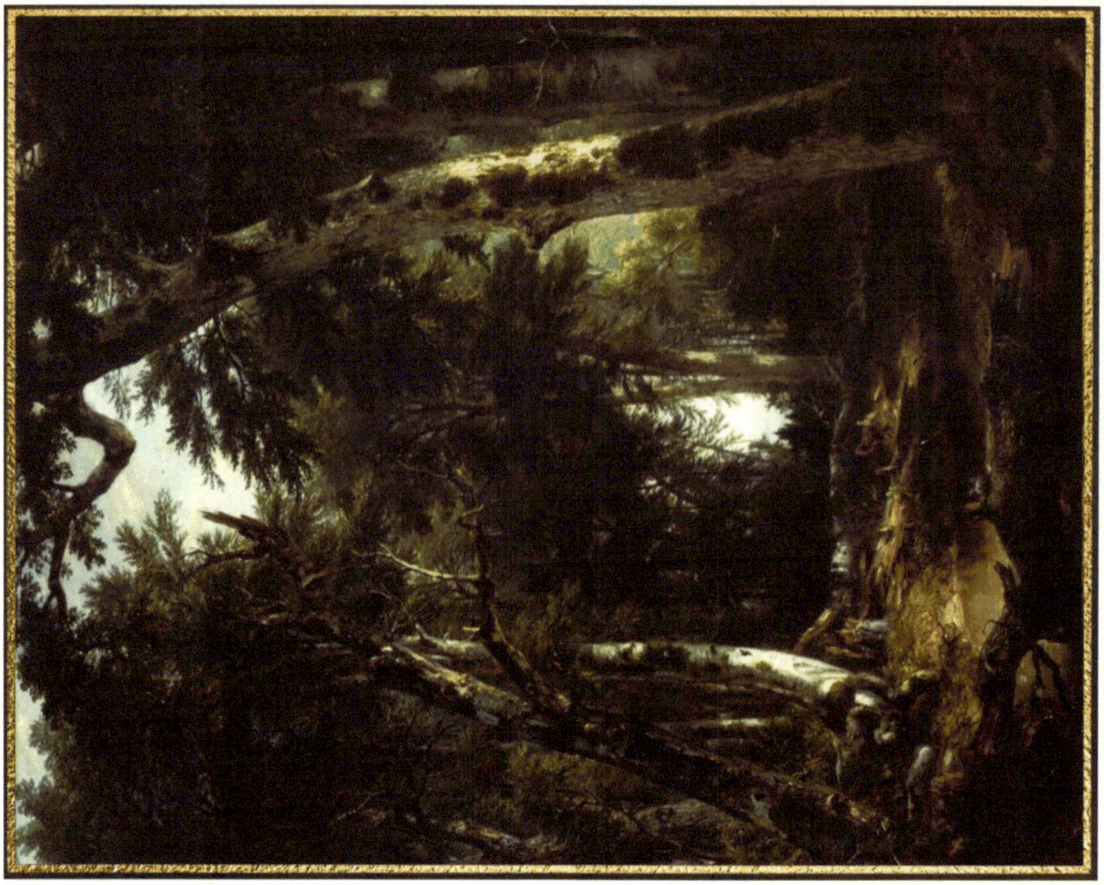

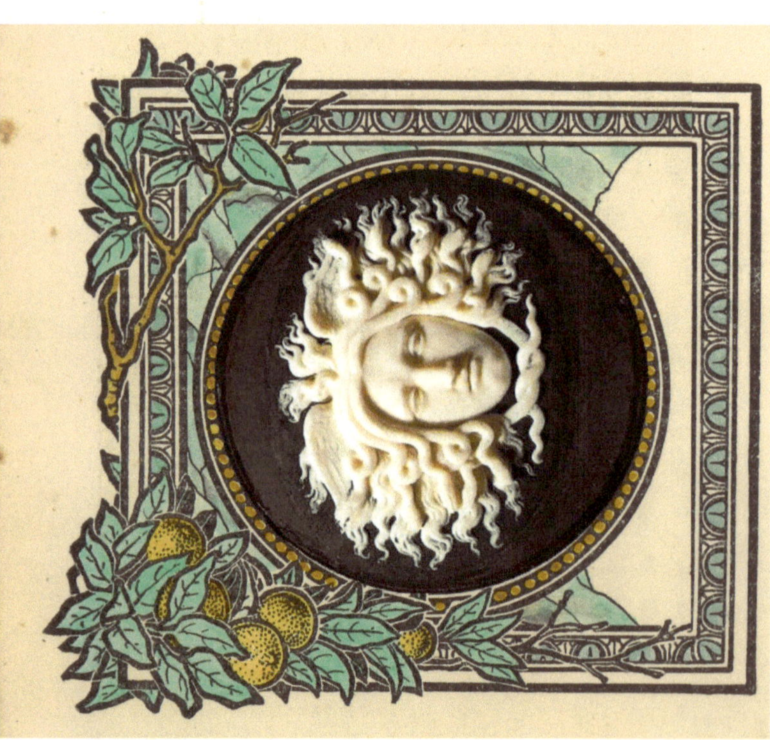

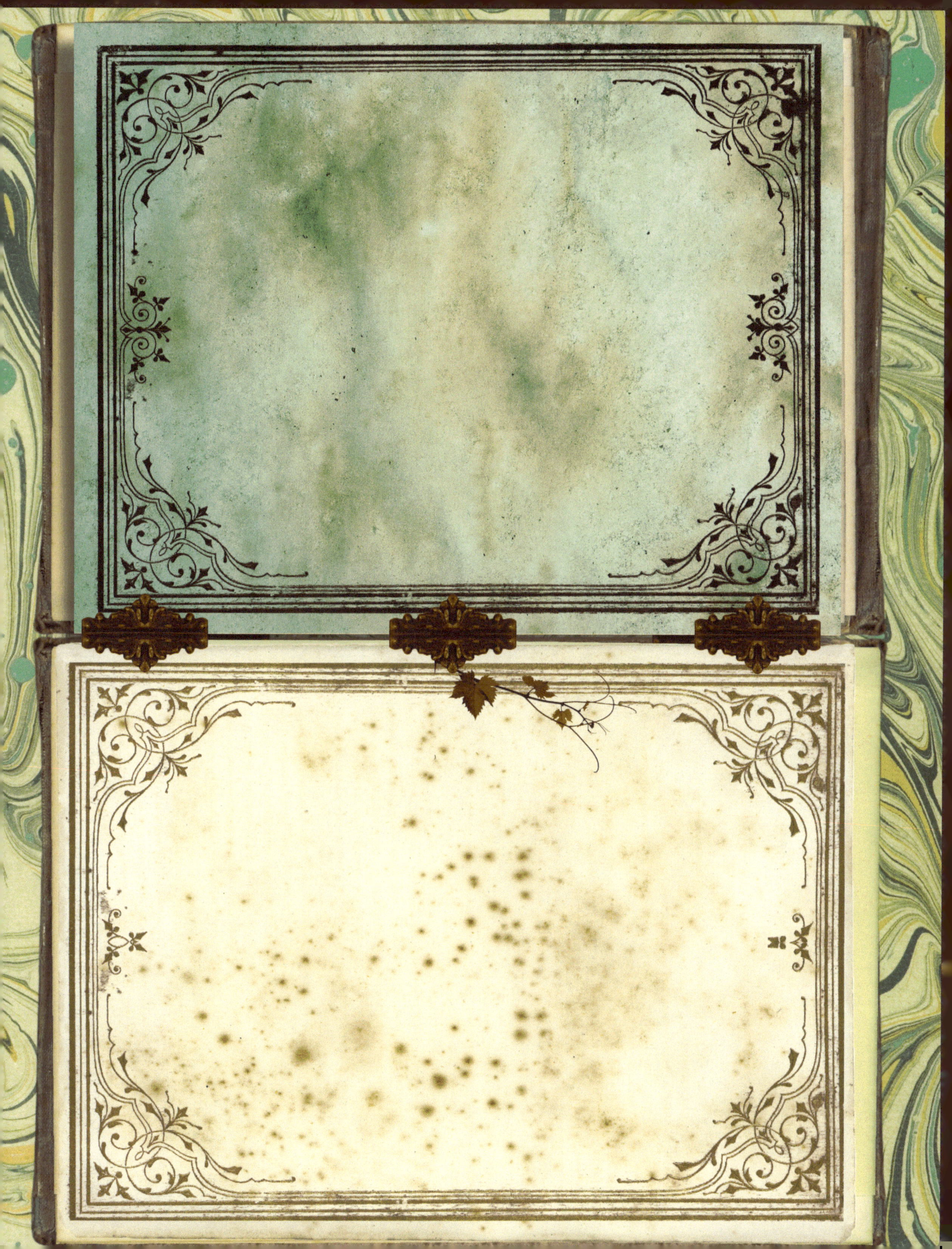

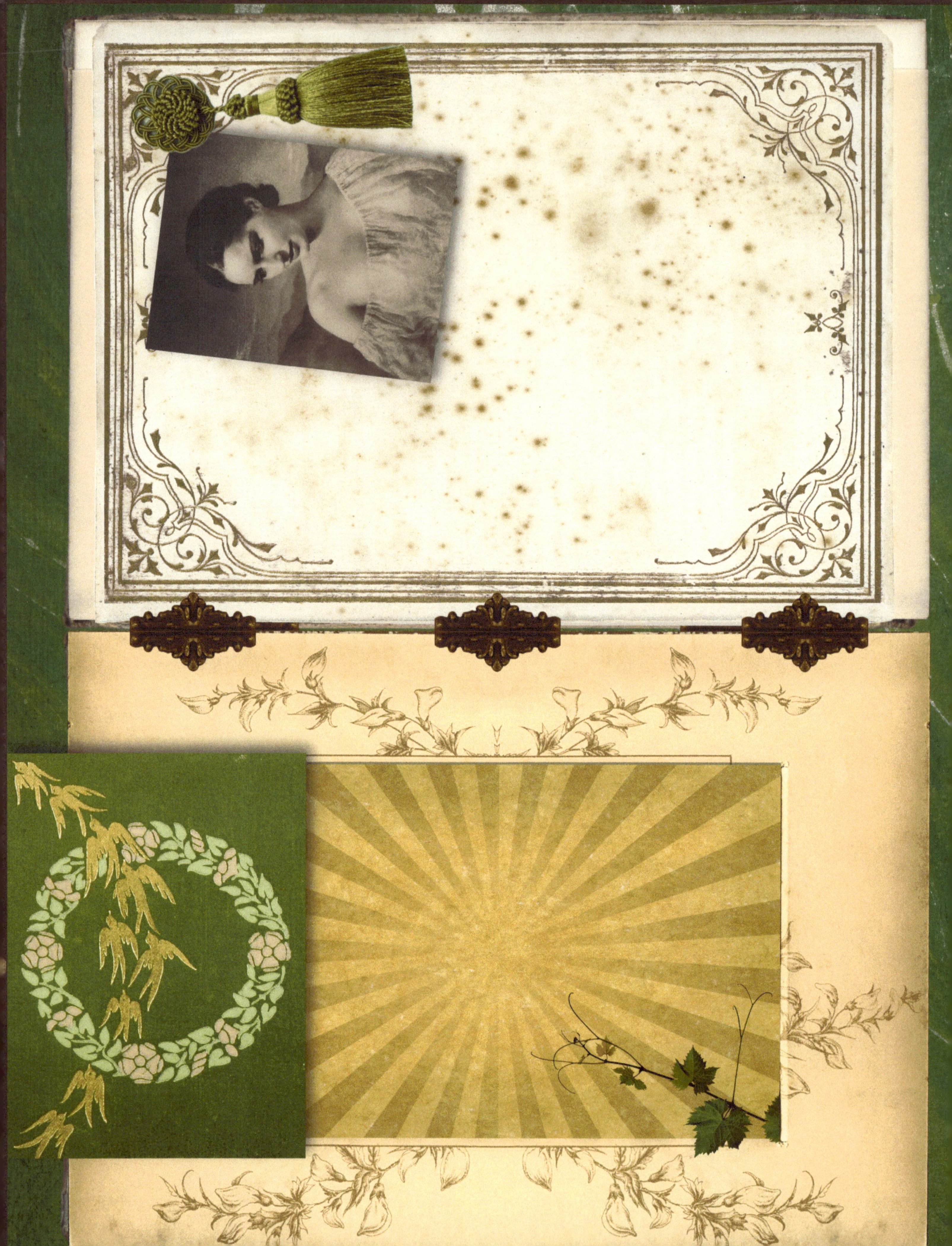

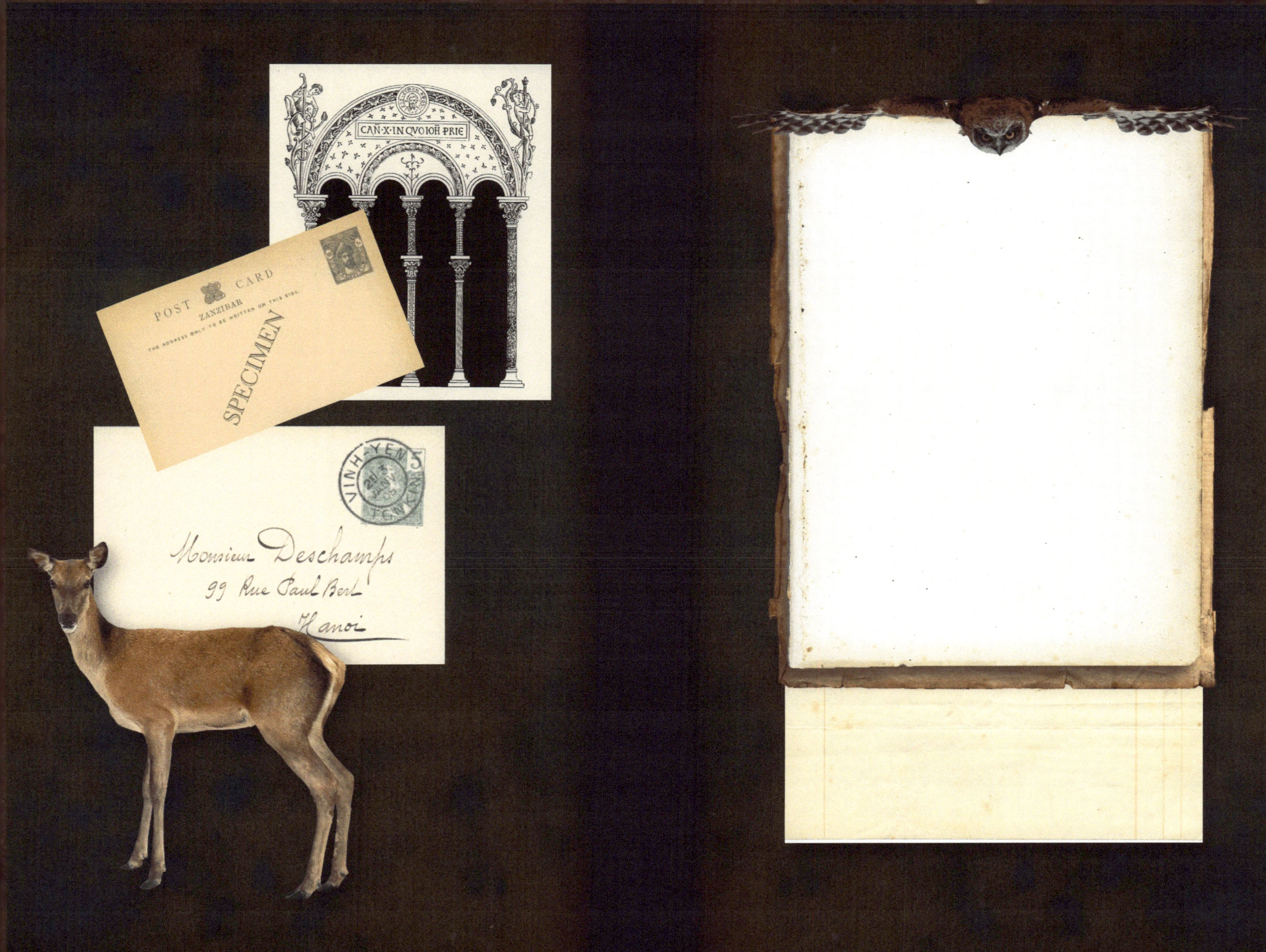

CAN·X·IN·QVO·IOH·PRIE
POST CARD
ZANZIBAR
THE ADDRESS ONLY TO BE WRITTEN ON THIS SIDE.
SPECIMEN
VINH-YEN
TONKIN
Monsieur Deschamps
99 Rue Paul Bert
Hanoi

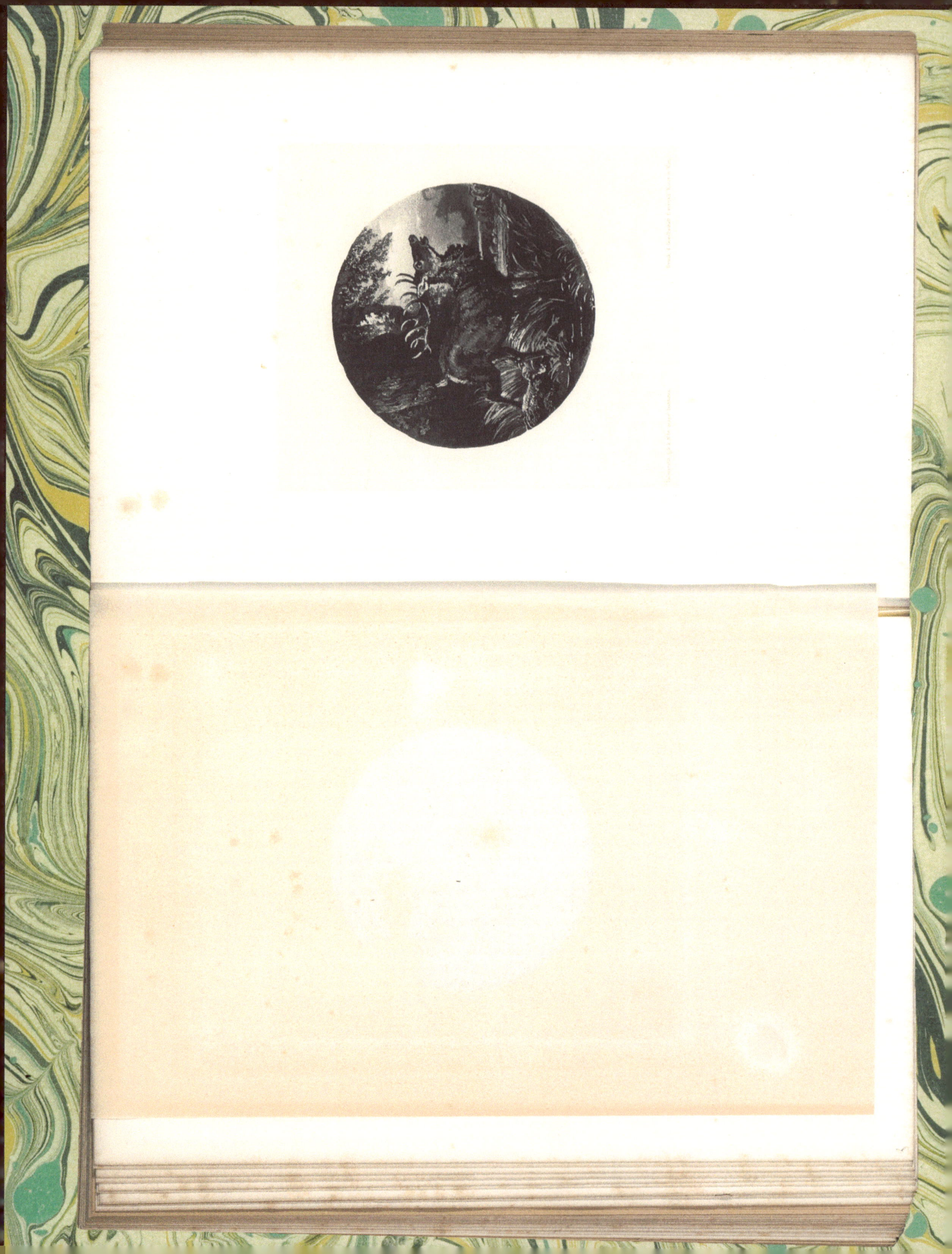

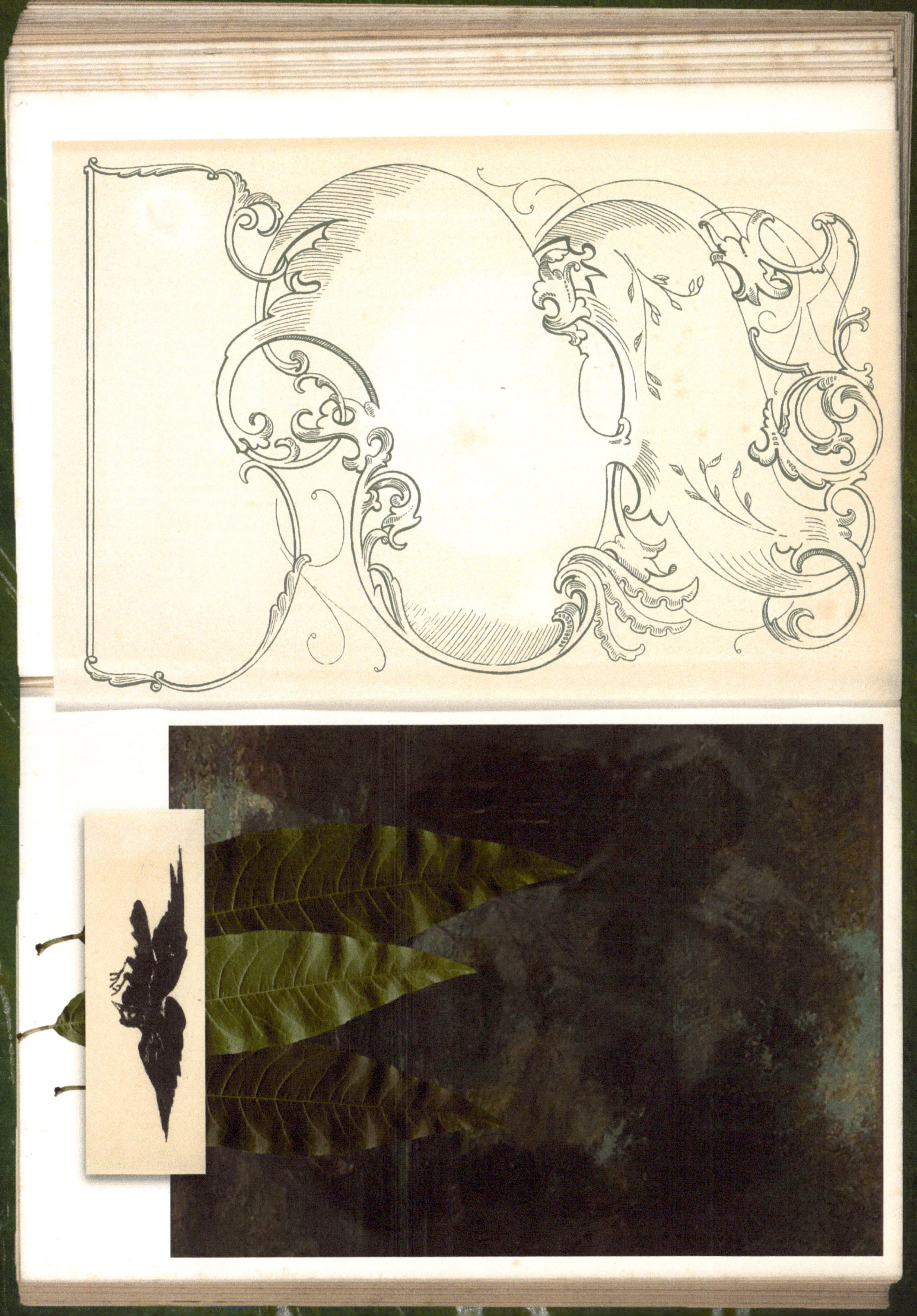

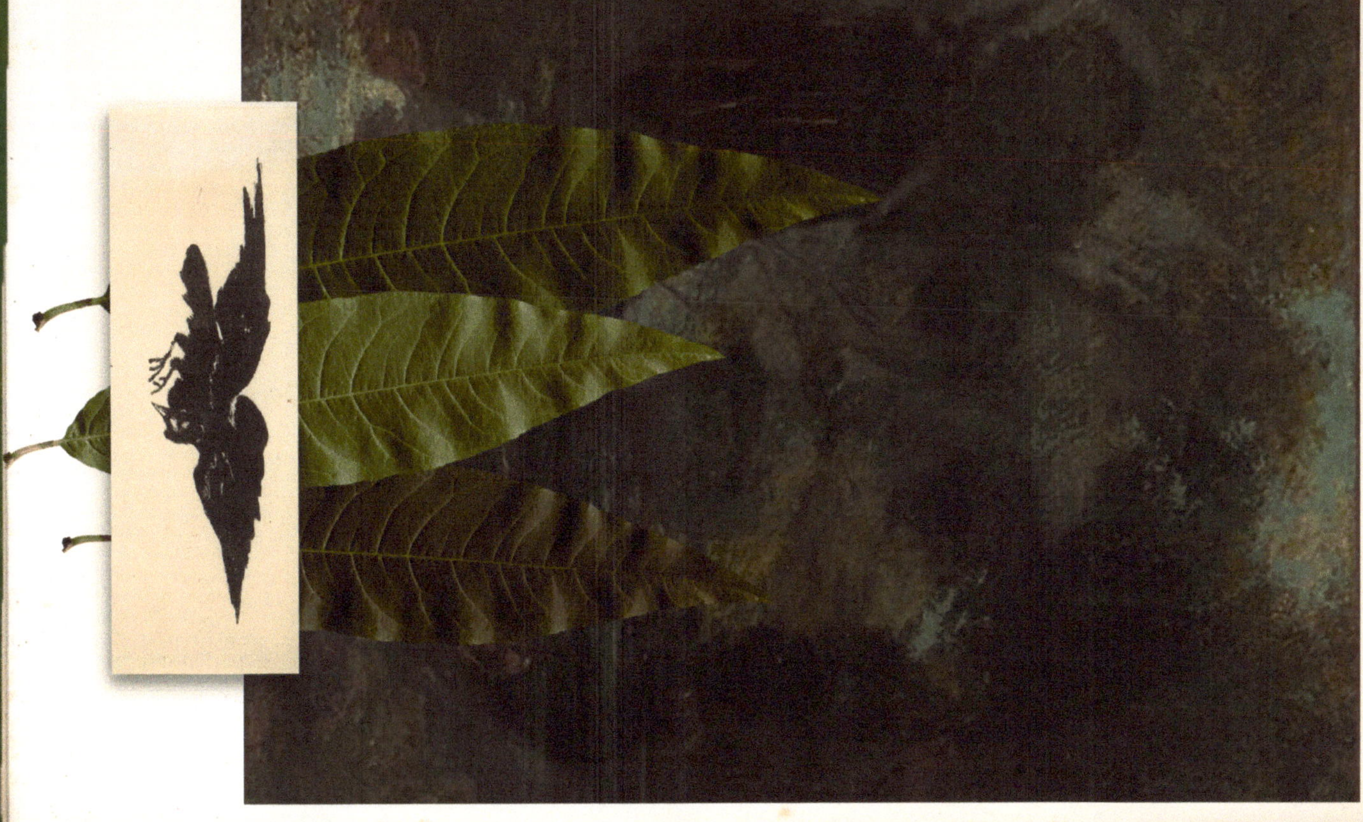

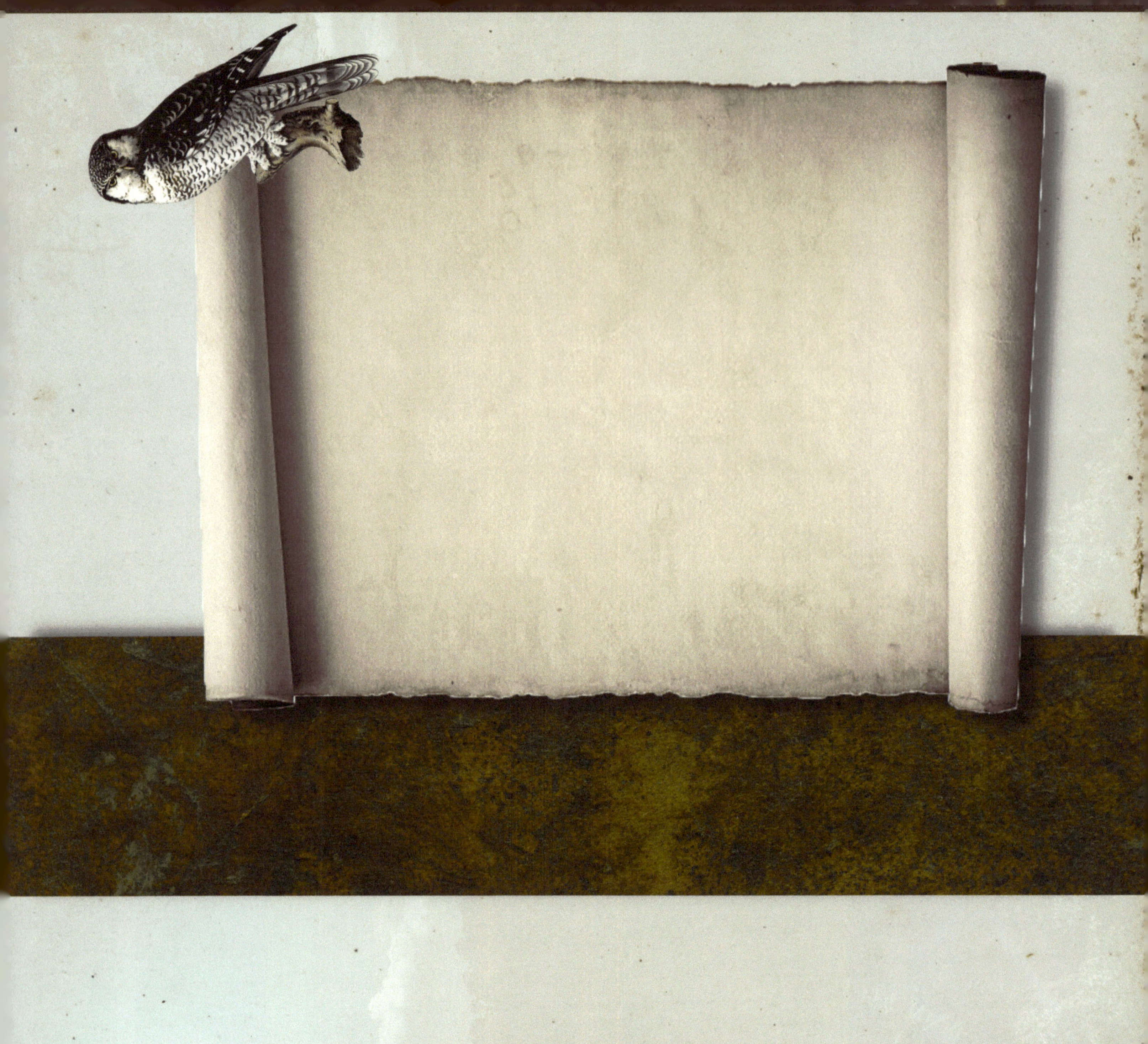

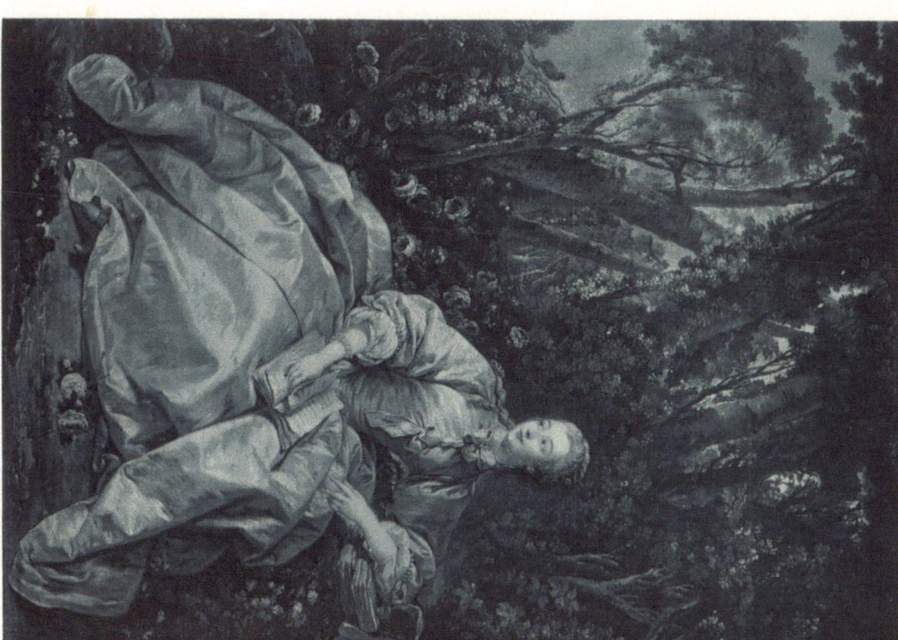

Madame de Pompadour

PHOTOGLYPTIE GOUPIL & Cⁱᵉ

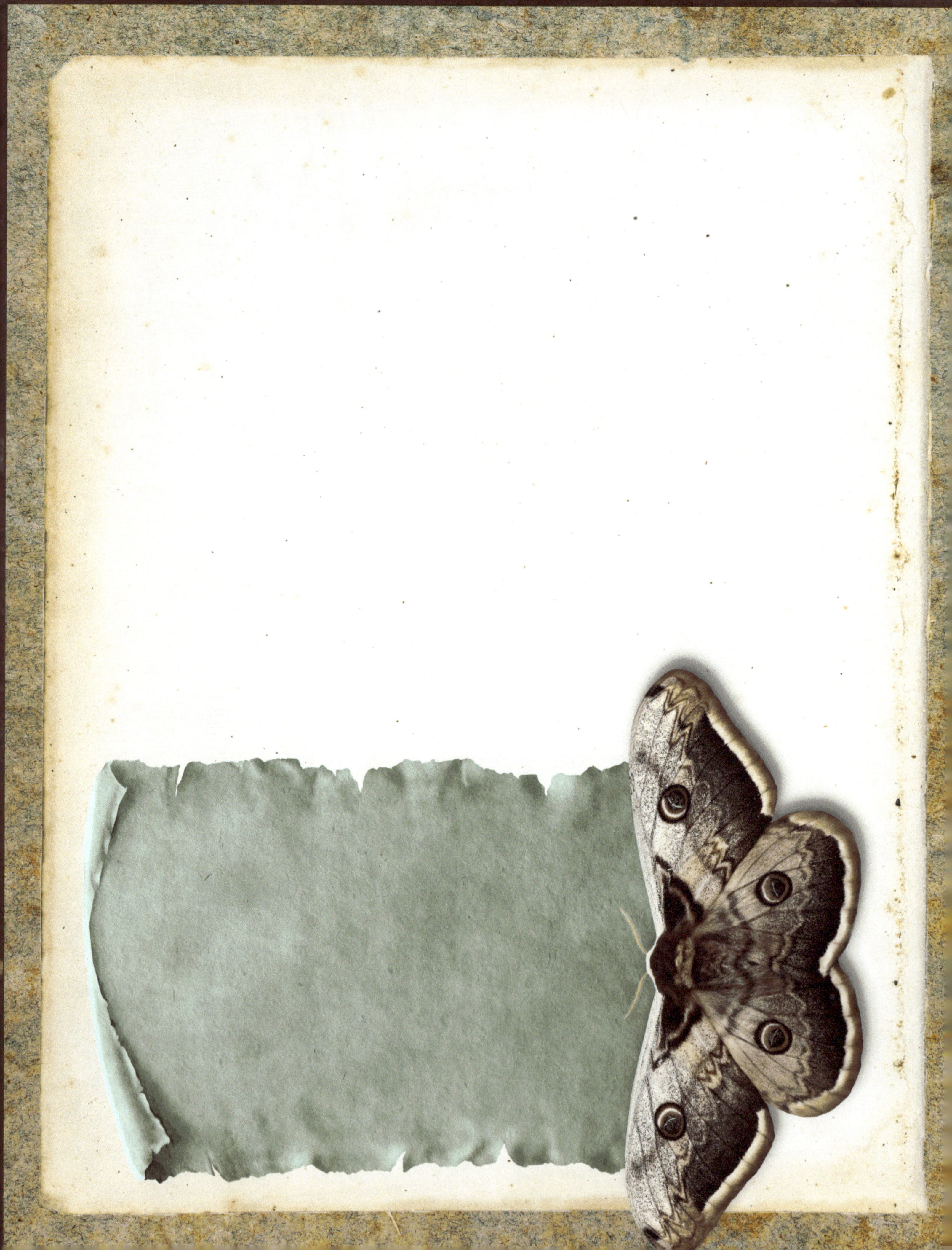

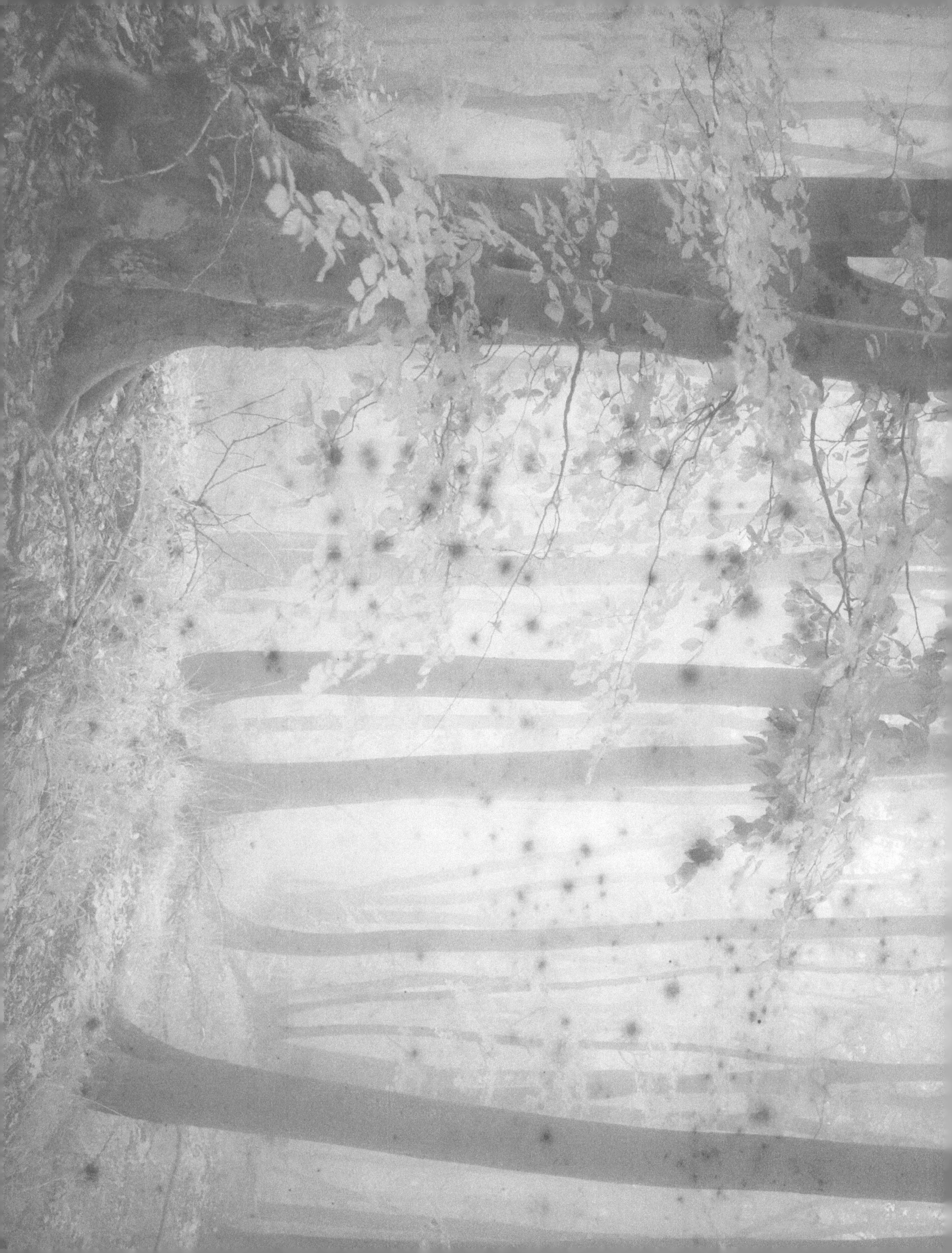

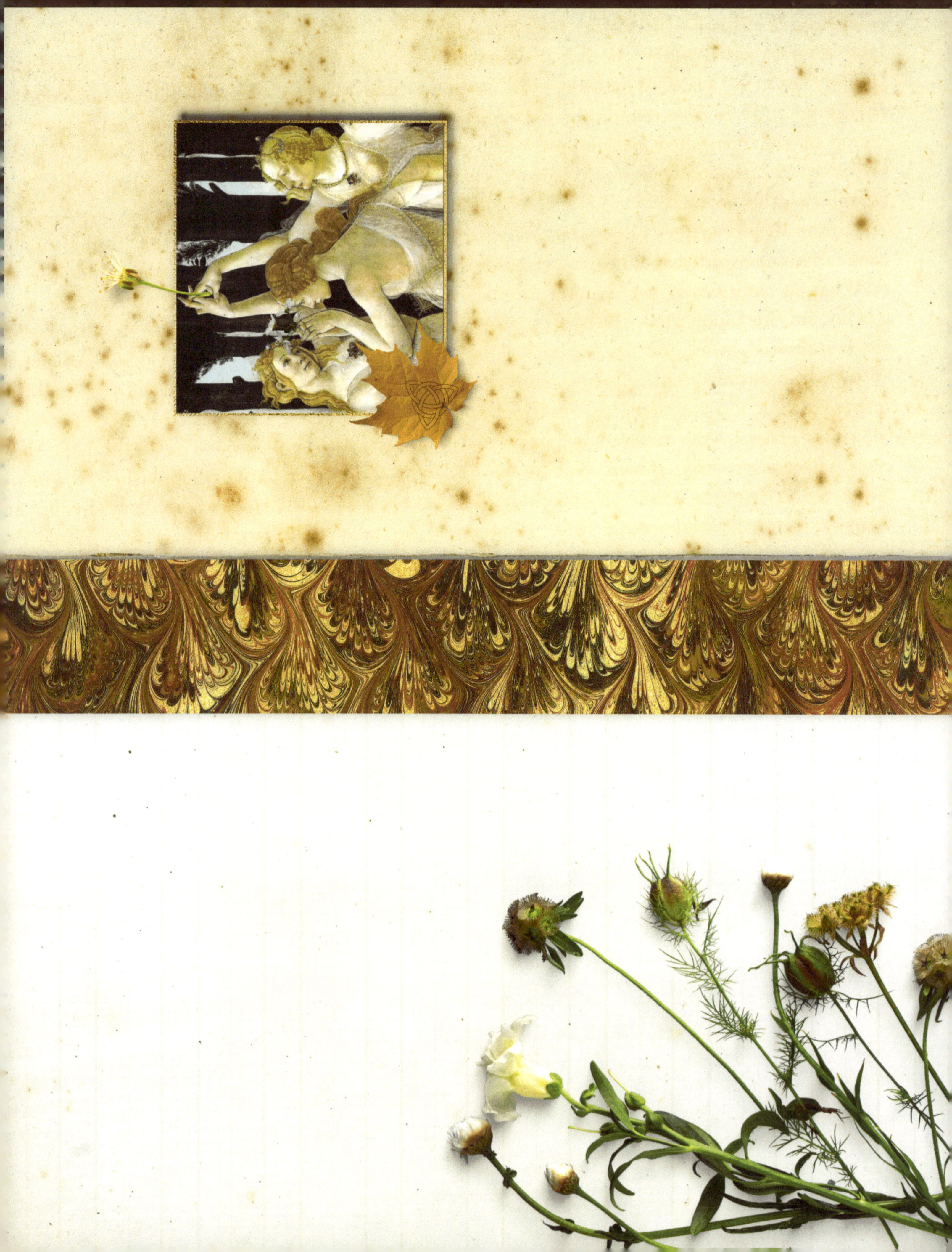

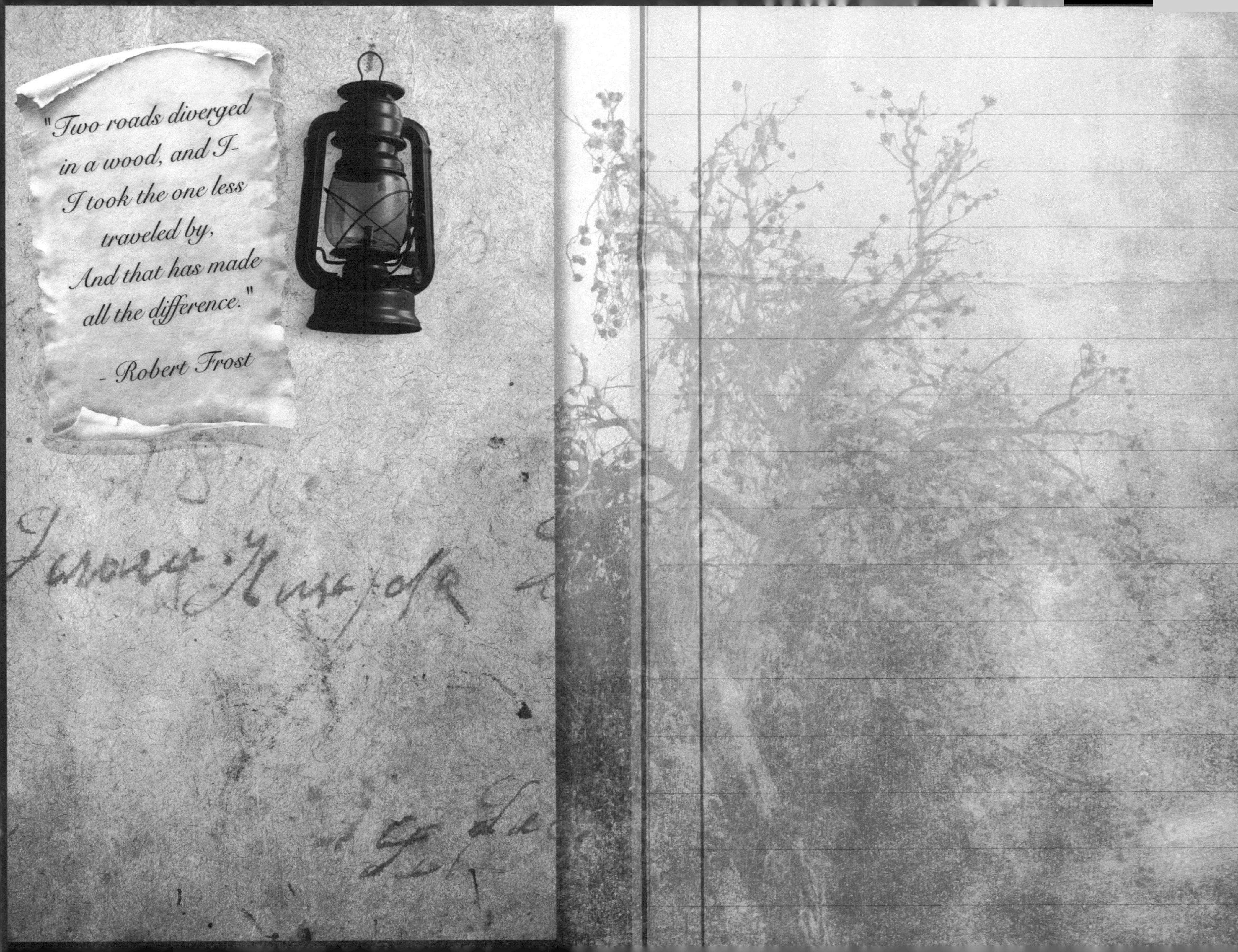

"Two roads diverged
in a wood, and I-
I took the one less
traveled by,
And that has made
all the difference."

- Robert Frost

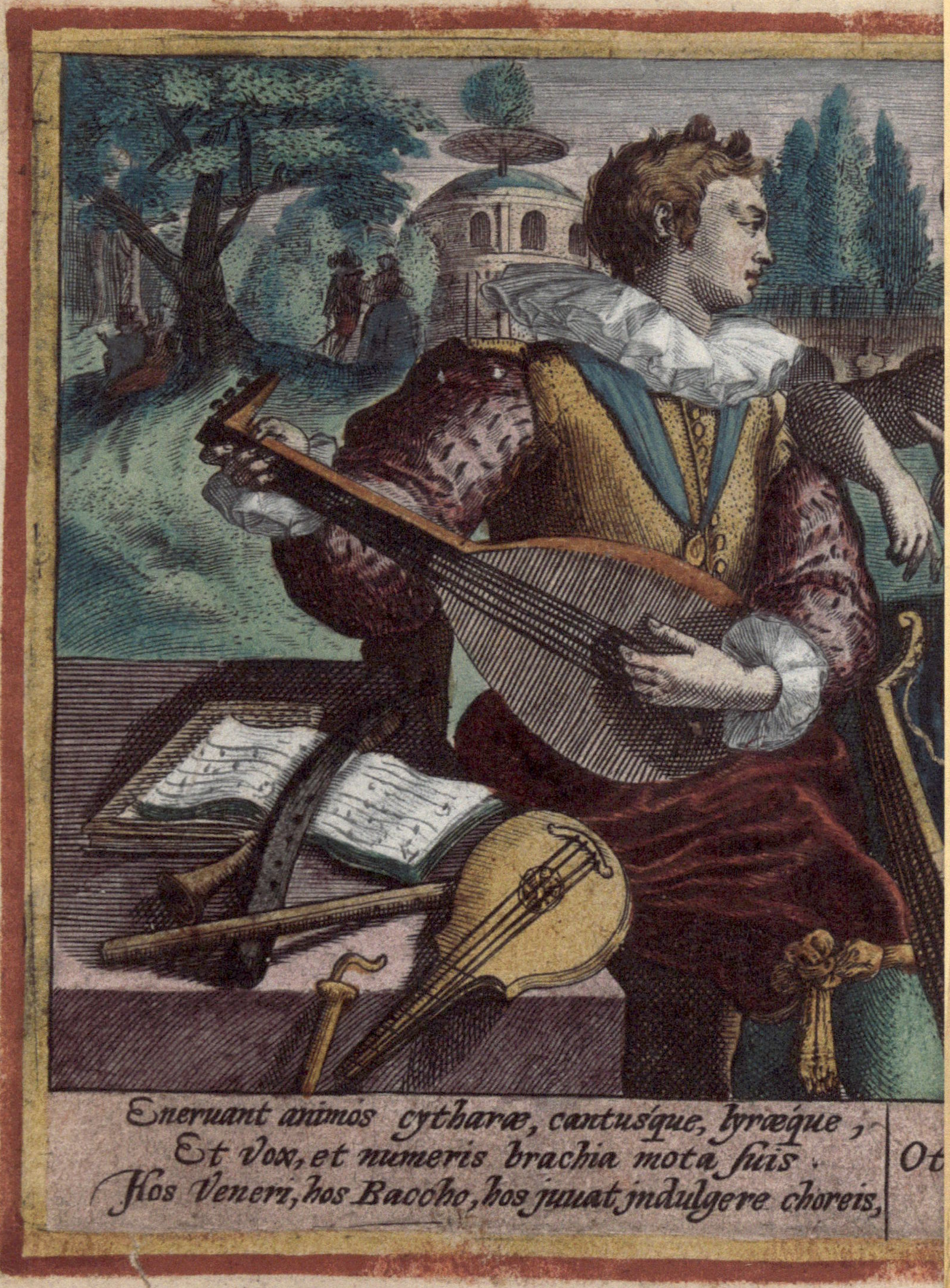

Eneruant animos cytharæ, cantusque, lyræque,
Et vox, et numeris brachia mota suis.
Hos Veneri, hos Baccho, hos juuat indulgere choreis,

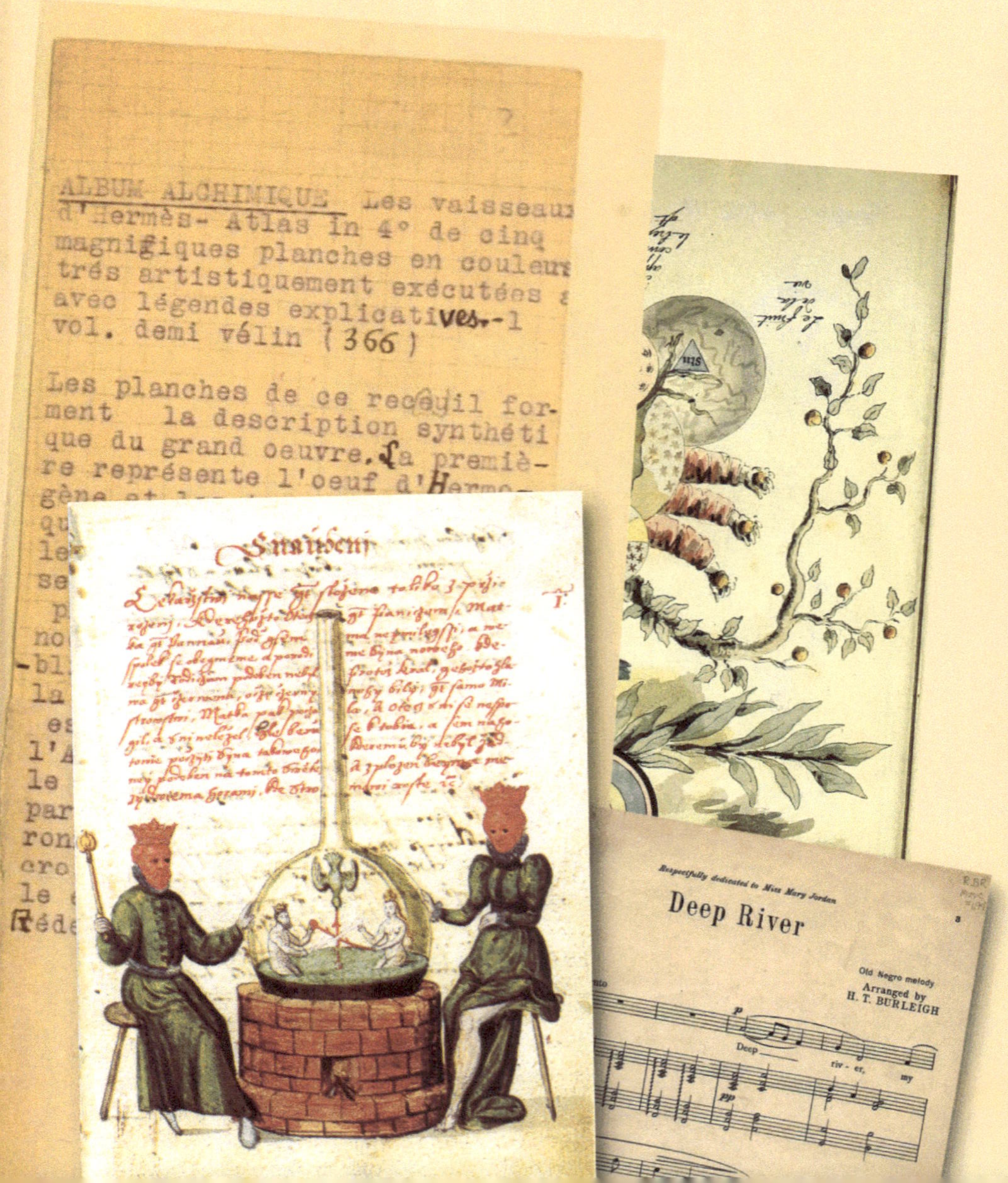

ALBUM ALCHIMIQUE Les vaisseau[x]
d'Hermès- Atlas in 4° de cin[q]
magnifiques planches en coul[eur]
très artistiquement exécuté[es]
avec légendes explicatives.-1
vol. demi vélin (366)

Les planches de ce recueil fo[r]
ment   la description synthéti[-]
que du grand oeuvre. La premiè[-]
re représente l'oeuf d'Herm[ès]

Deep River

Extrait Dell Registre

Vu par la Cour la requeste presenté
par le ... général du Roy contenant qu'il
a esté avis que le procès encommencé en la justice de
fontaine près vendôme aux nommés jean garreau le
jeune anneau pour raison d'excès et mauvais traitemens
exercés contre le nommé andré mesel, que le procès
avoit esté pareillement encommencé aud. garreau
pour raison d'un vol de bois fait dans la forest de
freteval lequel ledit garreau ayant esté decreté

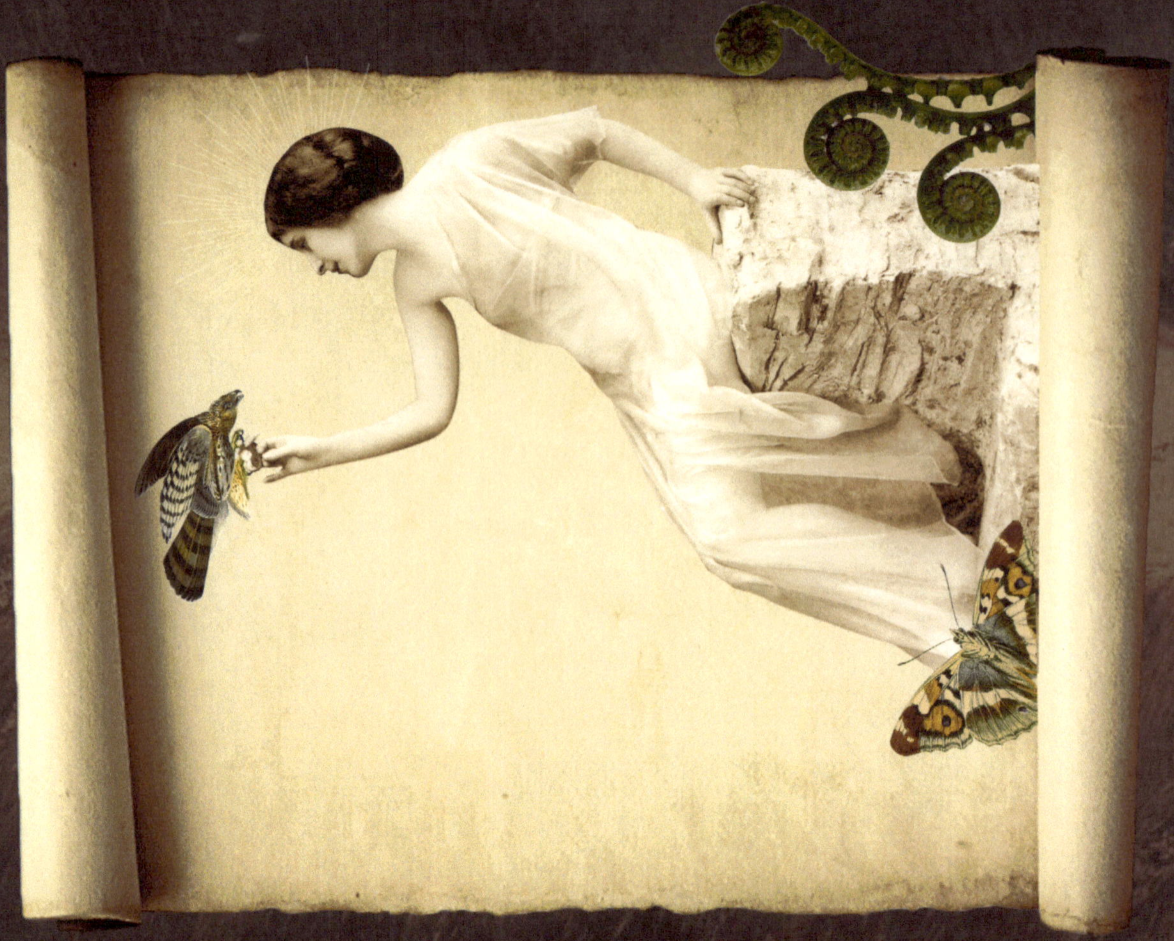

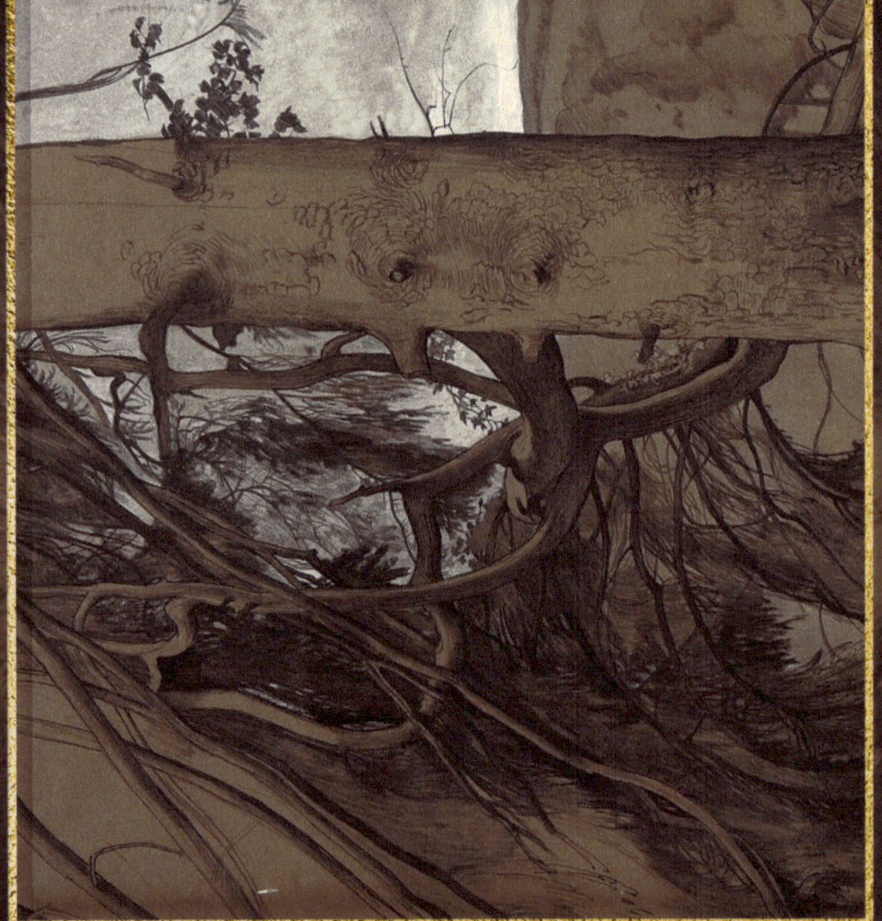

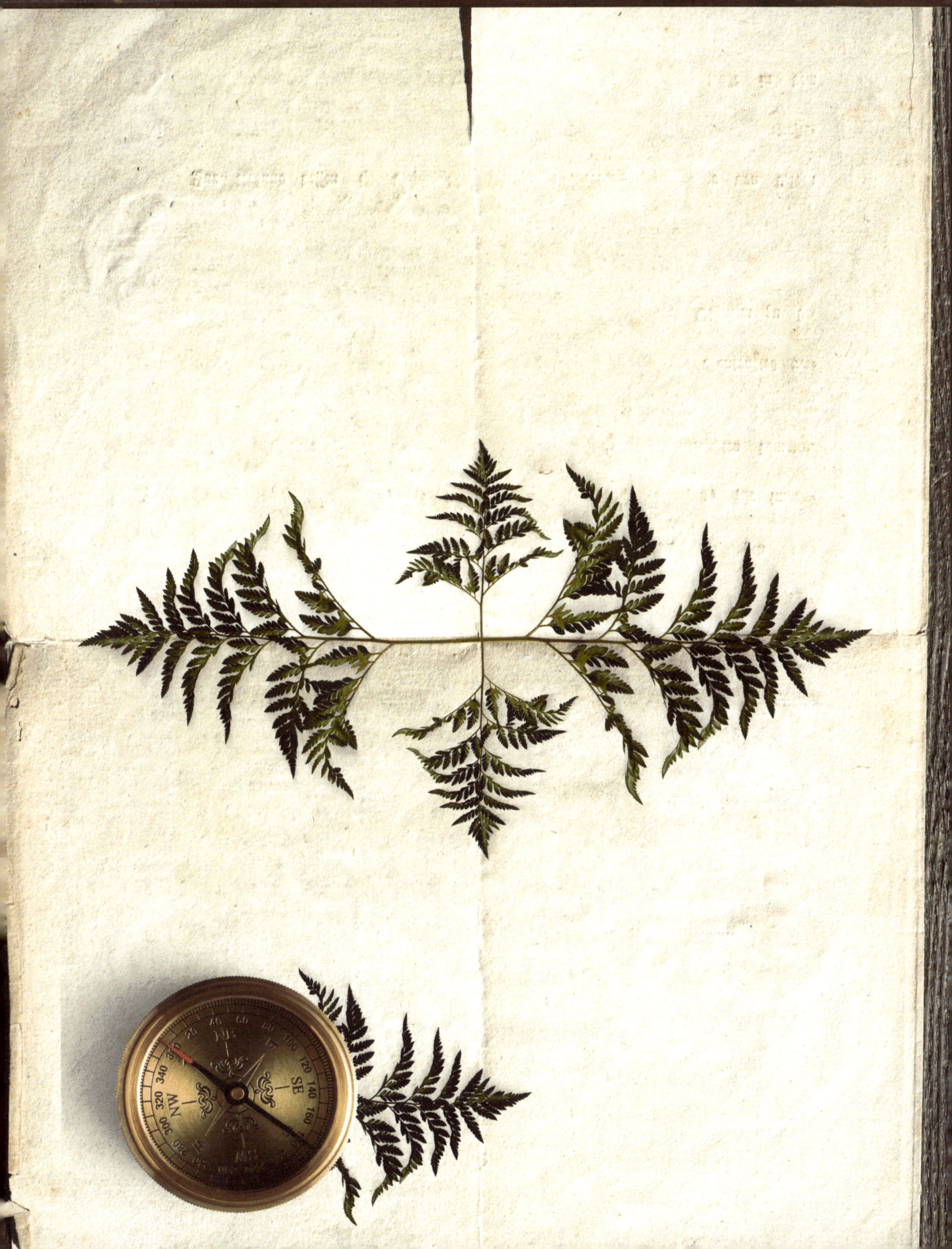

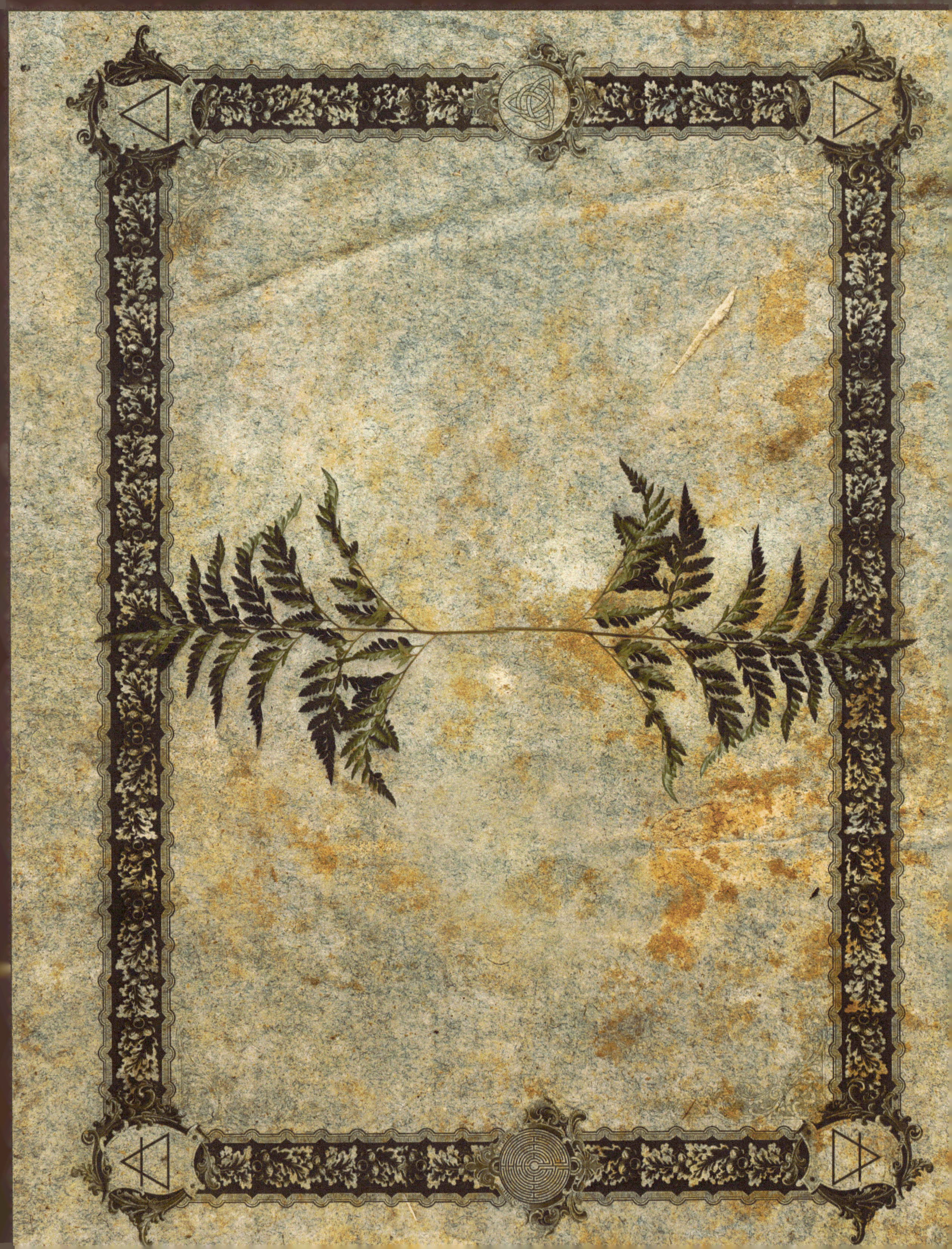

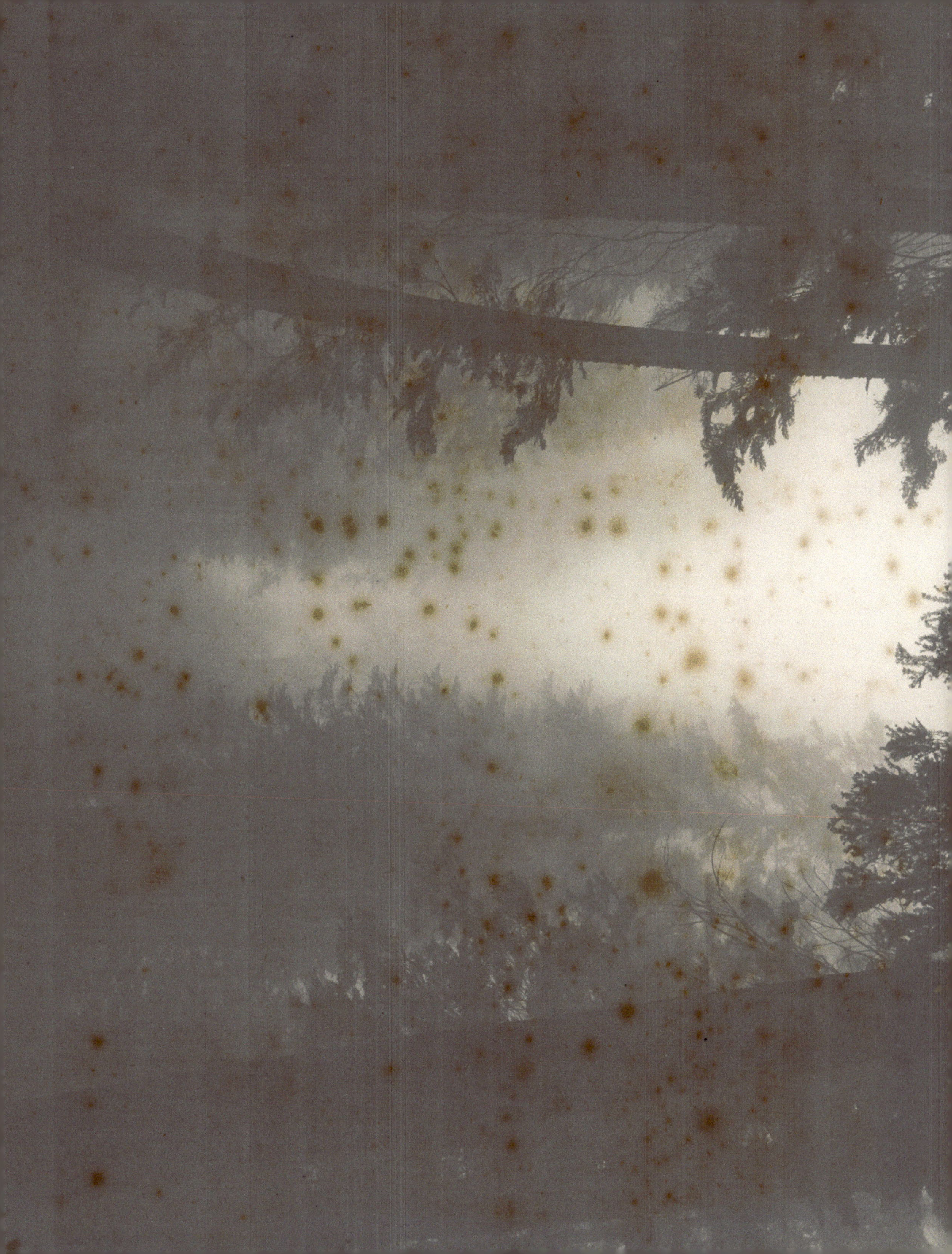

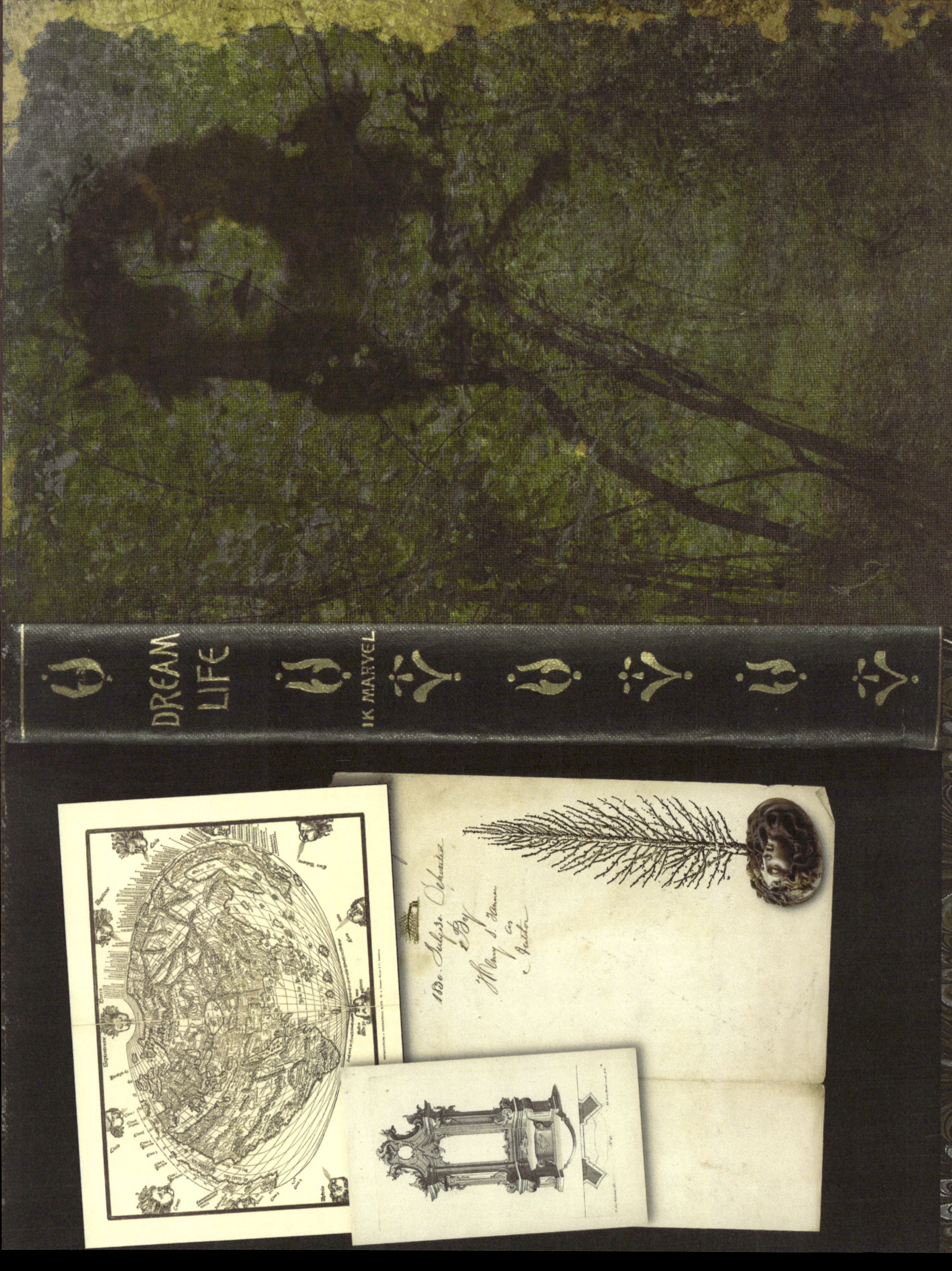

DREAM LIFE
IK MARVEL

Step 2

GROUP YOUR PAGES INTO *SIGNATURES*

Once you've gathered all the pages you want, sort your papers into groups of 4 pages (fig. 1). Each group of pages is called a **signature**. Each signature will be folded together as one.

If any of your page spreads are a full image that you want visible across both the left and right sides of the page, make sure that those are always on top of the pile, so you'll see the whole picture once each pile is folded in half. You can include as many *signatures* as you like. The more you have, the thicker your book's spine will be.

You can add in papers from your own collection, if you like. This is YOUR journal. If you have a lot of full-spread images, you can make more piles and add in extra papers under each one. Just make sure each centerfold image has at least 3 papers underneath it. These can be different thicknesses, special art paper, or duplicates of note pages printed from a digital kit. Once your piles are in the order you want them, you're ready to continue!

Take each group of pages, making sure they're all facing the same way (top to bottom) and fold them gently in half as a group. (fig. 2)
You can press along the crease to sharpen it, using a 'bone folder' or a spoon if you prefer a more orderly look. *If you want an extremely tidy look, you can go over the crease of each page individually.*

TIPS & NOTES

- **You will be able to see the outer papers along the spine.** If you want the spine of your finished book to have only one color of paper showing, with no print, use a blank sheet of paper on the bottom of each pile.
- We'll be creating a hard front and back cover. There will be a decorative, exposed spine, so we can show off a lovely *French Link* binding stitch. In case you're a pro and prefer a covered spine, I've included spine paper for you.
- **Unless you do not want to add a cover, we will be gluing the marbled endpapers to the first and last pages of the book, so make sure that the bottom paper in the first and last pile are pages you don't mind covering up.** You can add in an extra blank page to those signatures if you prefer not to sacrifice any of the designed pages.

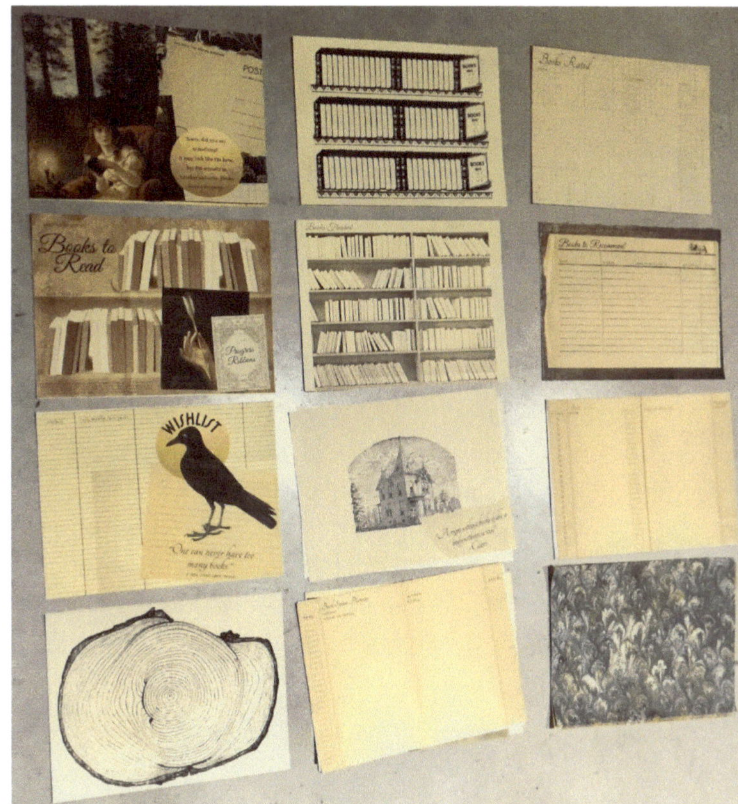

fig. 1 (above) *I have sorted my pages into 12 piles. You only need 4 piles for a standard junk journal, but I added a lot of extra blank drawing papers so I can sketch in my journal too. The page on top of each pile will be the centerfold of each signature.*

fig. 2 (below) *I have folded each signature in half.*

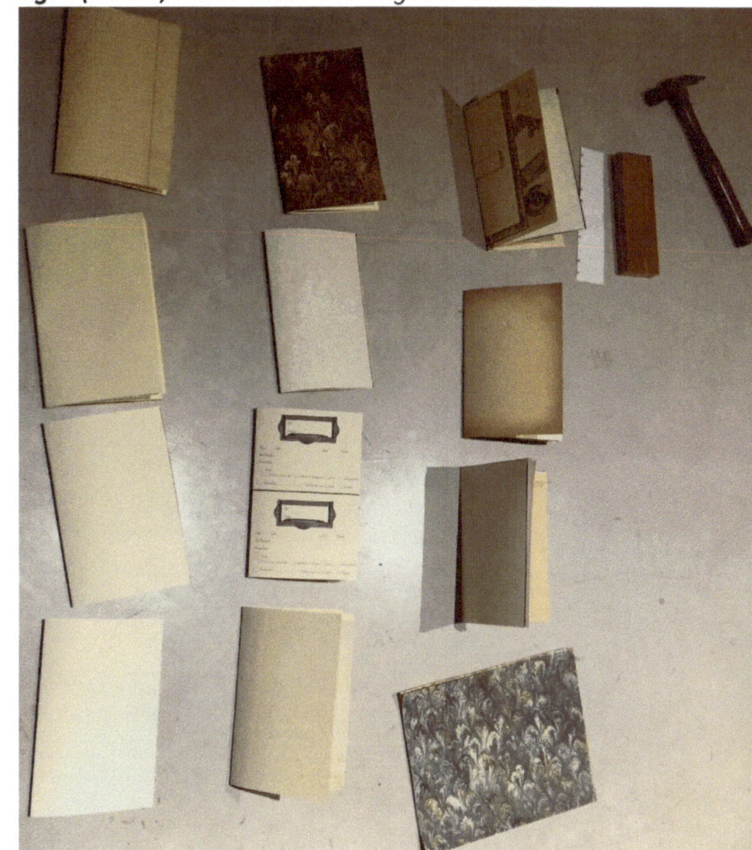

Step 3

The page after this one is called *The Crescent Moon Bookbinding Stitch Guide.* We're going to use it for step 3, so please cut it out of the book now, then come back here. *I'll put on some coffee and wait.*

In this step, we're going to sew your signatures together. First, let's poke holes along the folded line of each page grouping. My stitch guide isn't as fancy as the one you've just cut out, but it does the job. Your stitch guide (which you can fold in half now to crease it) is the same size as one page spread of your opened book. *If one edge is uneven, line it up along the top of the page, when measuring.*

Unfold one signature so it lays flat. Place a piece of wood underneath it to protect your work surface. If you don't have scrap wood, you can use an old cutting board. **Line the stitch guide up** with the top page so the holes align with the fold. Use an awl or any other pointy object to **poke holes** in the center of each circle on your Stitch Guide. Make sure the hole goes through all the pages in your signature.

Repeat until all of your signatures have holes.

Now place your folded signatures in one pile, in the order you want them for your journal. Starting to look a bit like a real book, isn't it?

Flip through each signature to see how they will look in the book. Make sure you're happy with your page order, and then we're ready to connect them all!

Here's a little preview of what you'll be learning. We're going to connect the signatures so that the spine of the book looks like this. It's actually much easier than it looks! I'll walk you through it step-by-step.

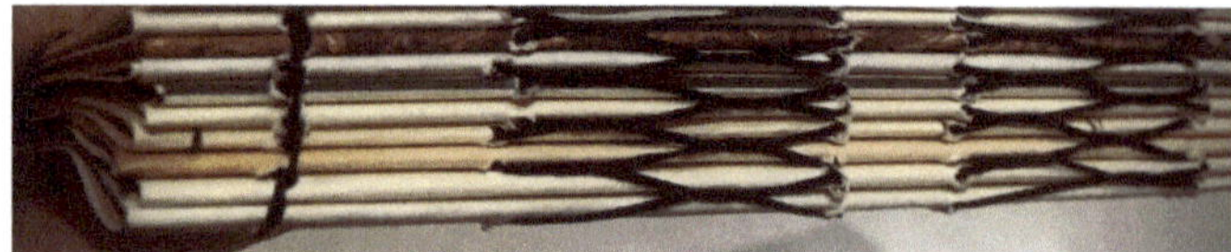

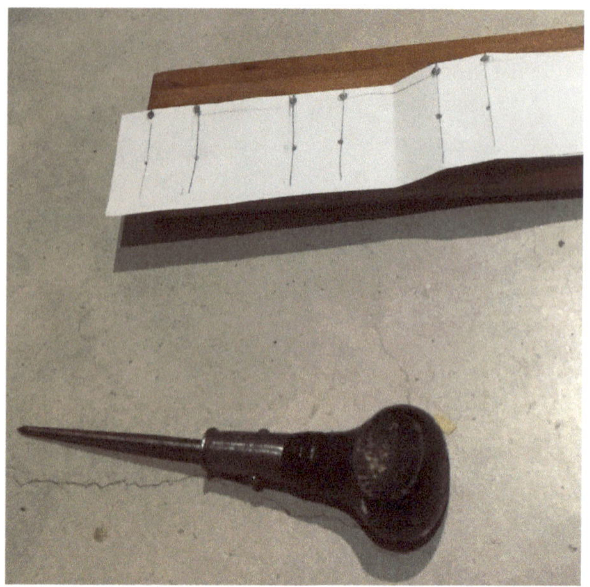

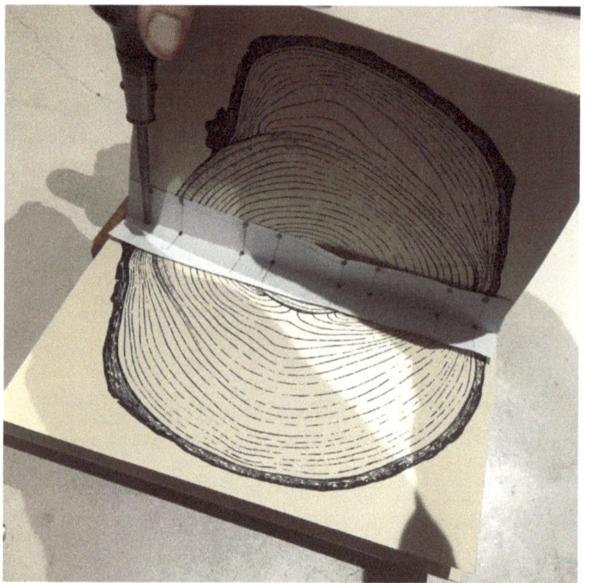

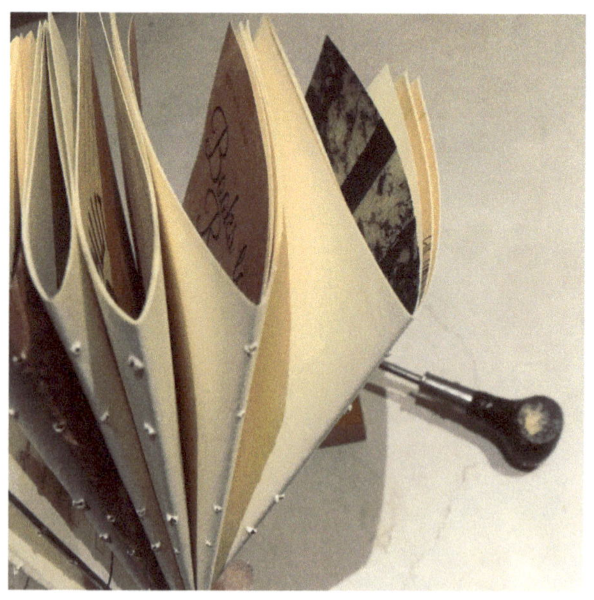

CRESCENT MOON

BOOKBINDING STITCH GUIDE

FOR THE

FRENCH LINK STITCH

1. FOLD THIS PAGE IN HALF ALONG THE CRESCENT MOON LINE.

2. PLACE IT IN THE CENTER OF A SIGNATURE (THAT'S A GROUP OF 4 PAGES THAT ARE FOLDED AT ONCE TO MAKE A SECTION OF YOUR BOOK).

3. USE AN AWL, OR ANOTHER POINTY OBJECT TO POKE HOLES IN THE CENTER OF EACH CIRCLE.

THIS WILL ENSURE THAT ALL OF YOUR SIGNATURES LINE UP SO YOU CAN SEW THEM TOGETHER NICELY.

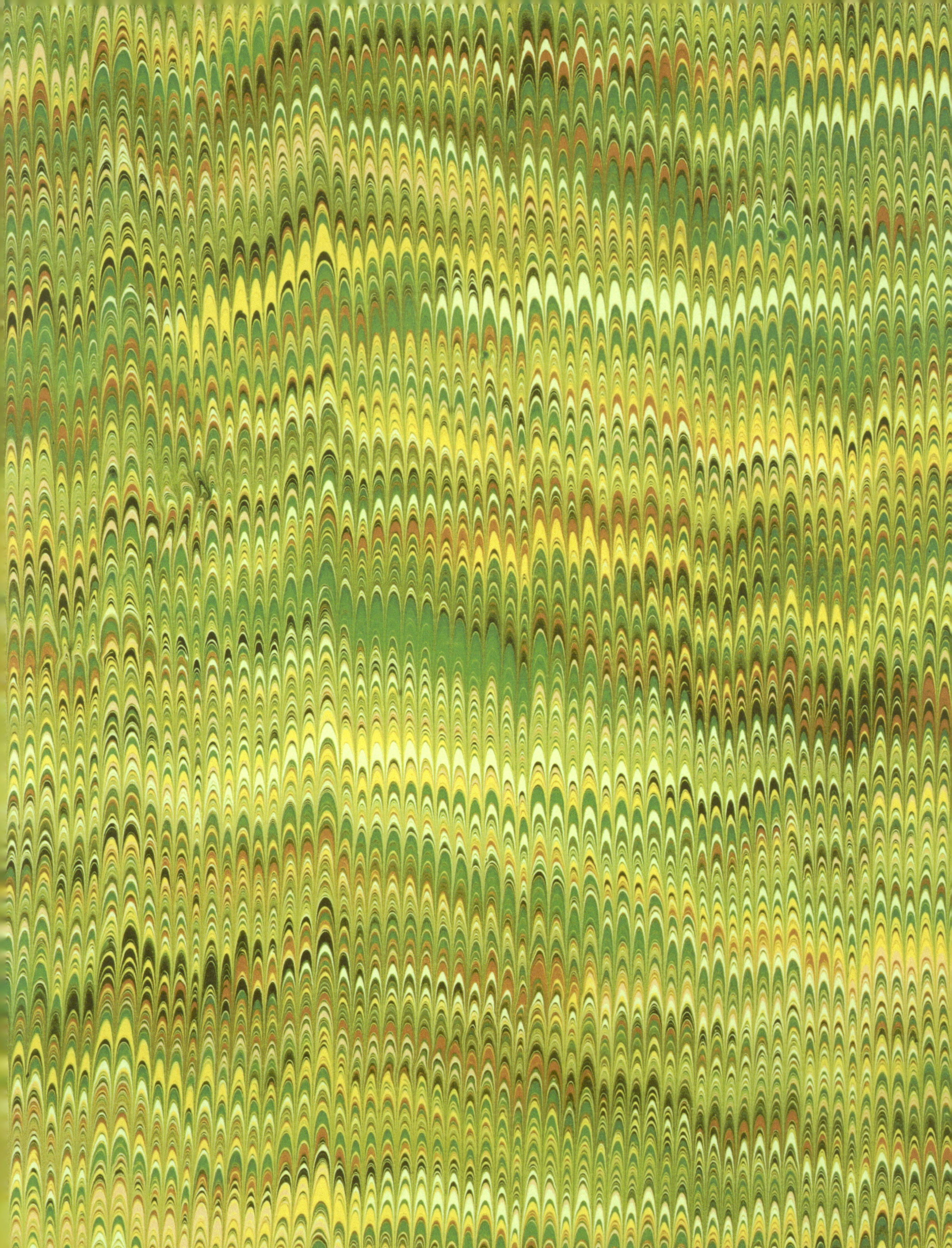

NOW IT'S TIME TO SEW OUR BOOK'S
INTERIOR TOGETHER.

First, let's cut a very long piece of thread. To figure out
how long your thread should be, count how many
signatures you have. *In the example below, I have 5
signatures.*

For every five signatures you have, add one extra
signature's worth of thread. Since I have 5, I'll cut a piece
of thread 6 times the length of my book's spine. So, if you
have 10 signatures, leave yourself enough thread for 12
times the length of your book's spine, and so on.

When you have your very long piece of thread cut, string it
onto a needle.

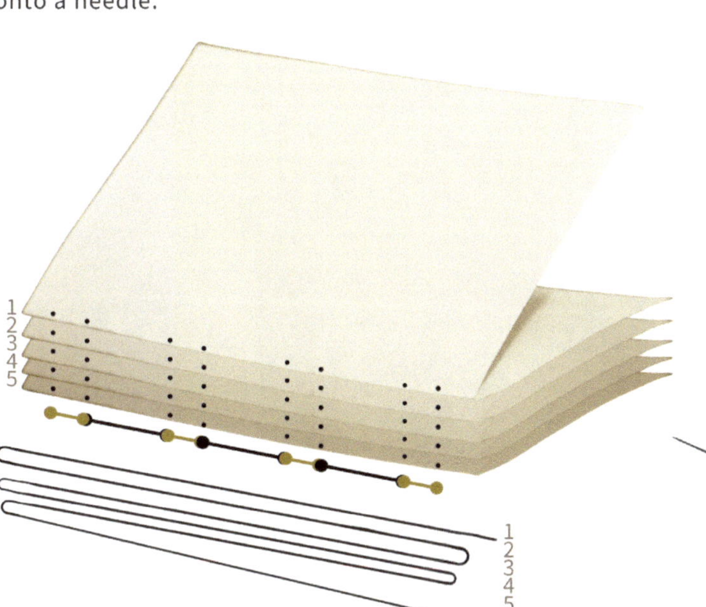

Here are some things to not worry about:

- *If your thread is too long, that's great! It's nice to have
  extra, just in case. You can always trim it at the end.*
- *If your thread is too short, you can always tie more on
  when you need it.*
- *If you put 5 pages instead of 4, or different paper
  thicknesses in some of your signatures, that's not a
  problem. The variety just adds to the intrigue.*
- *Second-guessing your choices and want a do-over? This
  magazine will be available for purchase as a digital
  download at **JunkJournalMagazine.com**, so you can
  print it out and make as many versions as you like. Keep
  them all or give them as amazing, handmade gifts!*

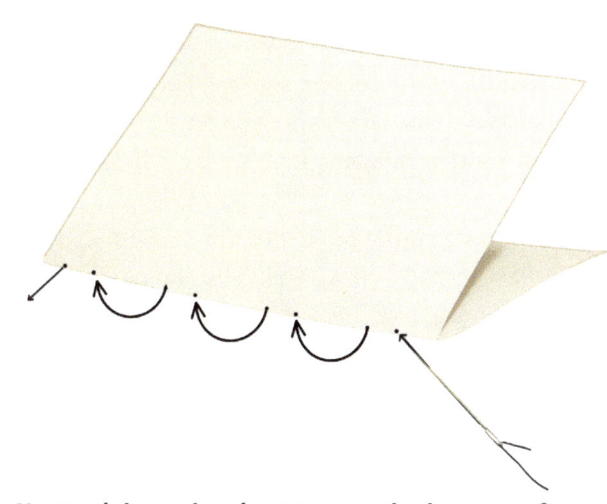

**Next, pick up the signature at the bottom of your
pile**
*(In the image to the left, that would be signature
#5the end of your book).* Take your threaded
needle, and starting on the outside/bottom of the
signature, sew into the center. Be sure to leave a
little 3" tail sticking out at the end. We'll need that
later on. Continue sewing out and in, through the
existing holes along the crease. It should look
something like this:

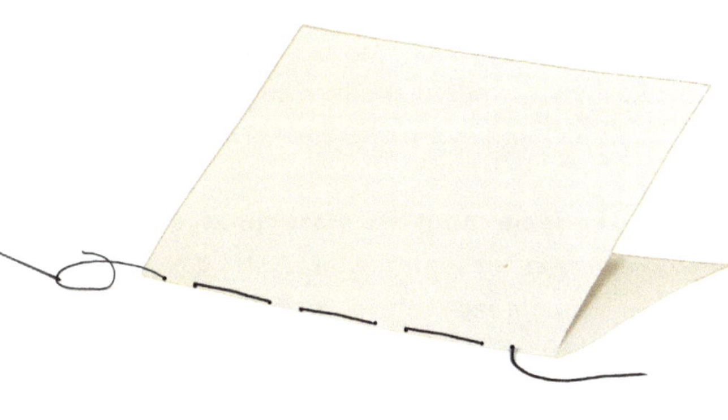

Now take the next signature from the back of your
book, and line it up on top of the one you just
sewed. Put the needle through the top hole of the
new signature, and out the next hole.

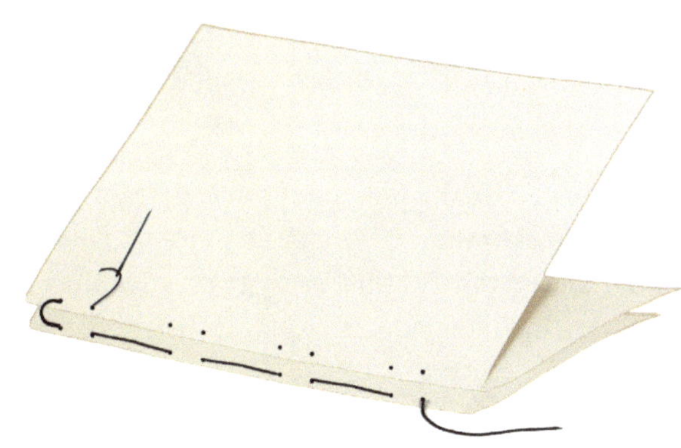

Now it's time to sew the first **link**. It's called a *link* because it links the current signature to the previous one. Just like links on a chain are connected, it simply loops through another link, and then goes on about its day.

Before putting your needle into the next hole, pass it behind the thread below. Then you can continue to sew in and out once, like this:

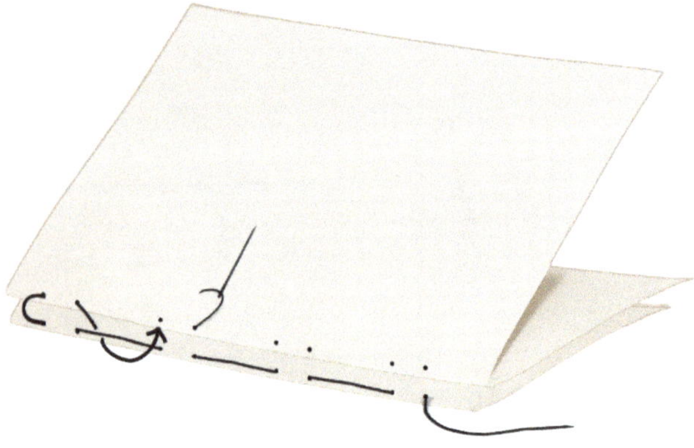

I see my friend walking along and I want to join her.
My friend is the thread already sewn into a straight path.
I catch up to where she is,
I am the moving end of the thread.
and I slip my arm under her elbow so we can *link up* and walk together. *And now we are linked! Magnifique!*

Let's do the same thing two more times, until the needle emerges through the last hole. Then, we'll gently pull the thread taut, so we can clearly see the first row of links.

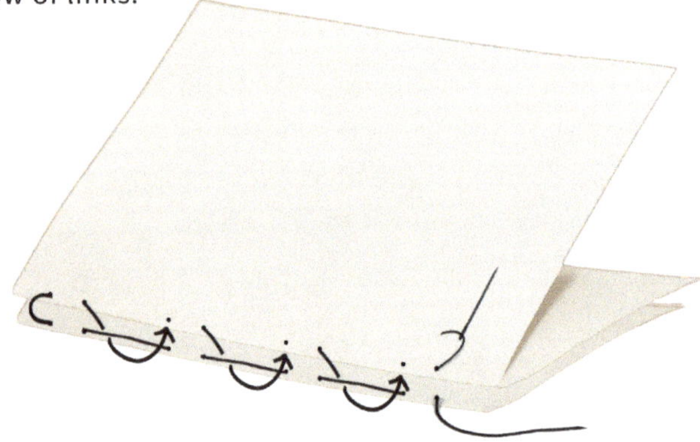

Now you can tie the tail end (from the beginning) to your **wandering thread**. [By *wandering thread*, I mean the end of the thread that is still free to go on adventures.]
You can tie it like this: Or like this:

After you tie the two ends together, if the eye of your needle is big enough, you can thread the tail through it, along with your *wandering thread*.

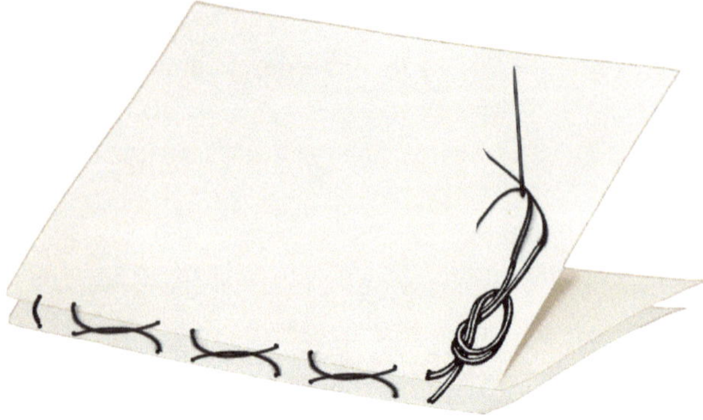

When we add on the next signature from the bottom of the pile, we'll pull both the wandering thread and the tail through the bottom hole, until the knot pops through to the middle of the signature. Let's do that now.

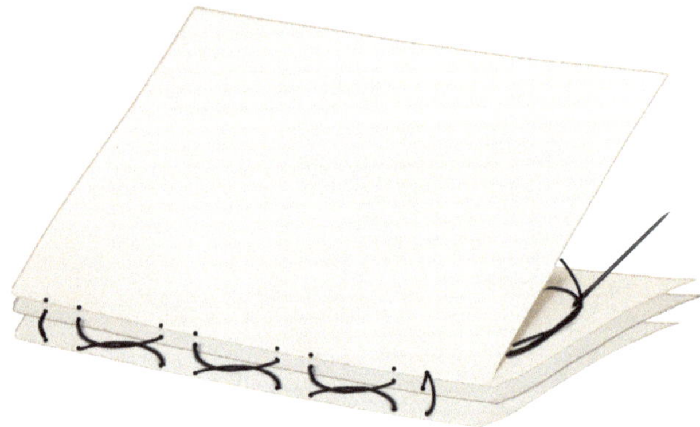

From inside the top signature, trim and tuck in the end of the tail. The wandering thread will stay in the eye (of the needle) to continue its journey. We will do another row just like before, with the French Link stitch.
I will not tuck my arm into my friend's elbow until the last possible moment of each stitch.

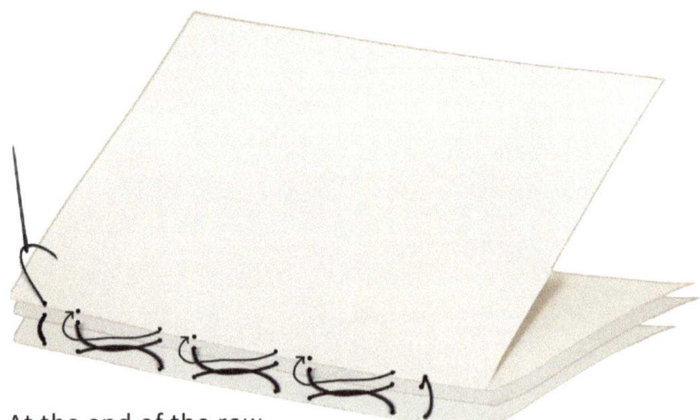

At the end of the row,
we will tighten our thread a bit, then connect it to the previous signature with a **kettle stitch**.

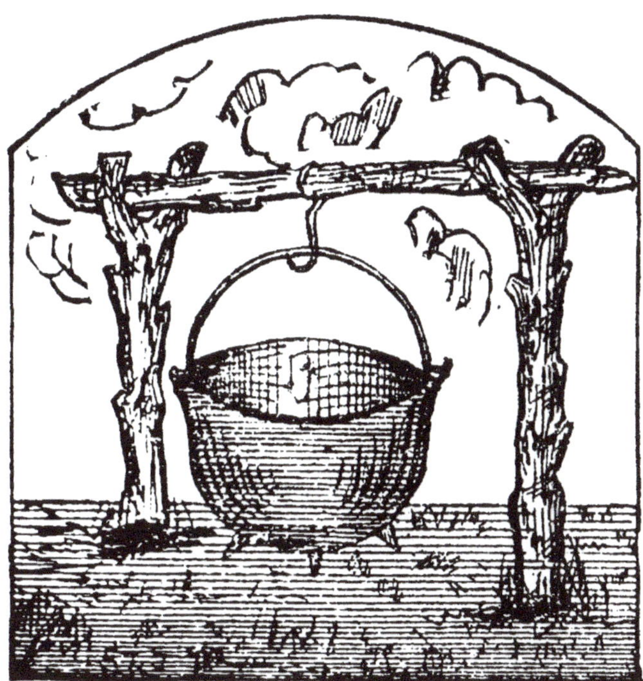

The Kettle Stitch

THIS STITCH CONTROLS THE TENSION ALONG THE SPINE AND BETWEEN THE SIGNATURES.

Like a kettle, this stitch is sturdy, but fairly simple. Before we begin, make sure that the thread along your current signature is as taut as you want it, so there are no loose bits hanging away from the spine. When you're ready, do the two steps below.

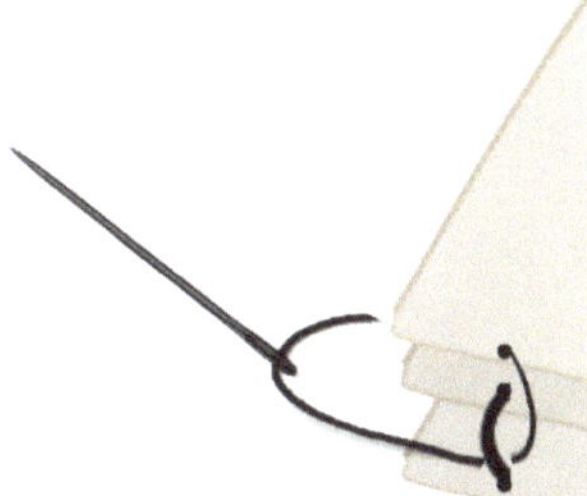

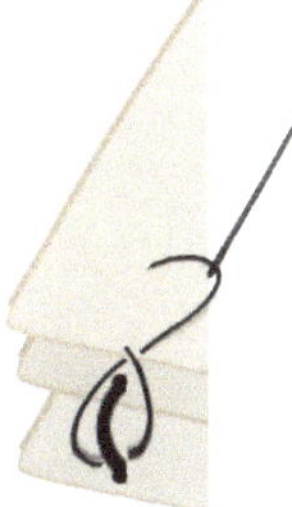

Step 1
Loop your *wandering thread* behind the stitch from the previous signature.

Step 2
Pass your needle behind where this stitch started. *Doesn't it look like a kettle would, if viewed from above?*

Tighten the kettle stitch to the desired level of tension and you can be on your merry way, passing the needle into the next signature.

Continue attaching all of your signatures together, using the two stitches you've already used. Use the *French link stitch* to travel up and down the spine, and the *kettle stitch* at the end of each row.

TIPS & NOTES

- **Try to keep the tension similar all the way along the spine.** If the *French link stitch*es are much looser than the *kettle stitches*, your book's spine will pinch in at the top and bottom.
- **Avoid making the kettle stitches too tight.** Some people like to pinch the spine 1" below where the kettle will be to fan the edge out, before doing the kettle stitch. If you hold it that way while you 'put on the kettle' you can be sure there's a decent amount of space between the ends of the signatures. This is particularly helpful in junk journaling, because it's likely you'll be stuffing these pages with all sorts of ephemera and treasures. That will add some serious bulk to your book! So leaving a bit of extra room in advance is similar to building a house with a guest room. You can easily accommodate any new arrivals you may wish to invite in.

After the last kettle stitch is done, pull your thread back through the hole, to the inside of your signature. Tie it securely to the binding thread next to it and trim the excess. Voila!

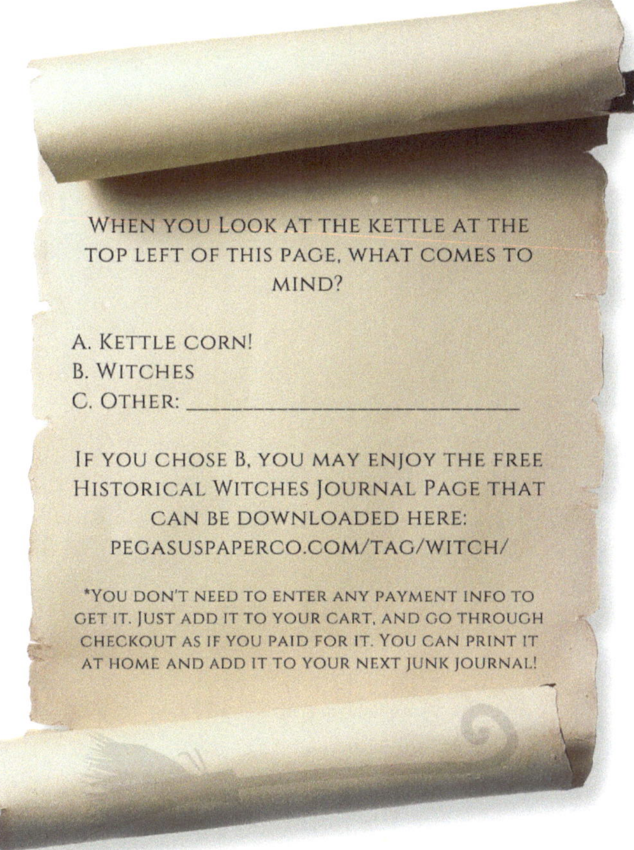

Step 4

MAKING THE COVER OF YOUR JOURNAL

Cut out the book cover designs. Then cut the covers off this magazine. They are decorated with marbled endpaper, which will be visible when you open the cover.

Use the size guide on the next page to cut out two pieces of cardboard for the book covers. A manila folder, a cardboard box... even a cereal box will do!

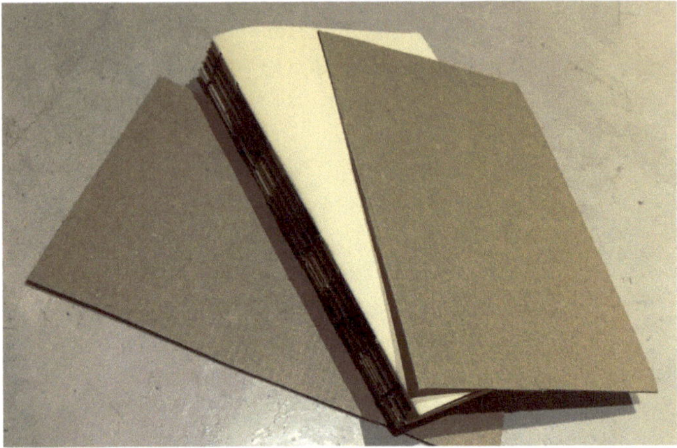

Place your cover image, *centered*, under the cardboard. Go ahead and fold those edges up around the cardboard, clipping any overlapping areas at the corners. *Always check the size and alignment before cutting, and protect your work surface before you glue anything.*

GLUE THE CARDBOARD BEHIND THE BOOK COVERS
Place thin strips of double-sided tape along the edges of the cardboard. Before peeling off the tape backing, press the tape firmly into the surface.
If you don't have double-sided tape, you can just use glue.

Use a large glue stick to apply glue on every part of the cardboard that doesn't have tape. Then peel off the tape backing, and firmly press the cover design into place, flattening out every surface. *If you have a rolling pin or brayer, this is a great way to flatten out any bumps.*

Now you can gently fold one of the longer flaps around the edge and (double-sided) tape or glue it down. **Choose the long side that will be touching the book's spine.** Do this for both covers. Now the paper on each cover should *cover* one side of the cardboard, and wrap around, along the spine-edge.

A BRIEF NOTE ABOUT GLUE: Different geographic locations have different sorts of glue, and they react to paper and ink differently. When in doubt, a glue stick and double-sided tape, or very thinly applied (not too wet) craft glue are fairly safe options. If you're using glue, you can test it by applying a small amount to the back of the "spine cover" page to make sure it's safe to use it. You'll know if it's too wet because the image on the reverse side of the paper will start to bleed or become discolored. If that happens, see if using an even thinner amount solves the problem.

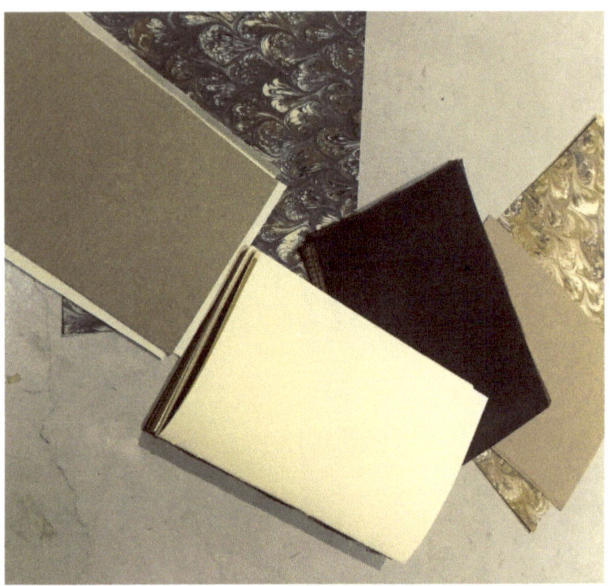

You may notice that I chose mismatched endpapers... I like writing instructions more than I like following them.

TIPS & NOTES

- **Would you like to have a ribbon in your book, to use as a page-marker?** Even though we aren't covering the spine, you can still have one! See the back cover of your book? On the side with the cardboard still showing, glue 2-3 inches of a long piece of ribbon along the wrapped-around paper edge, so most of the ribbon sticks out from what will be the top of your book. (I'm using a vintage *picot ribbon*. Velvet, satin, silk... all are lovely options.)
- **You should still have three paper flaps sticking out from each cover, not yet glued down.** If you do not want the wrap-around edges of the cover paper to show inside your finished book, glue them all down now.

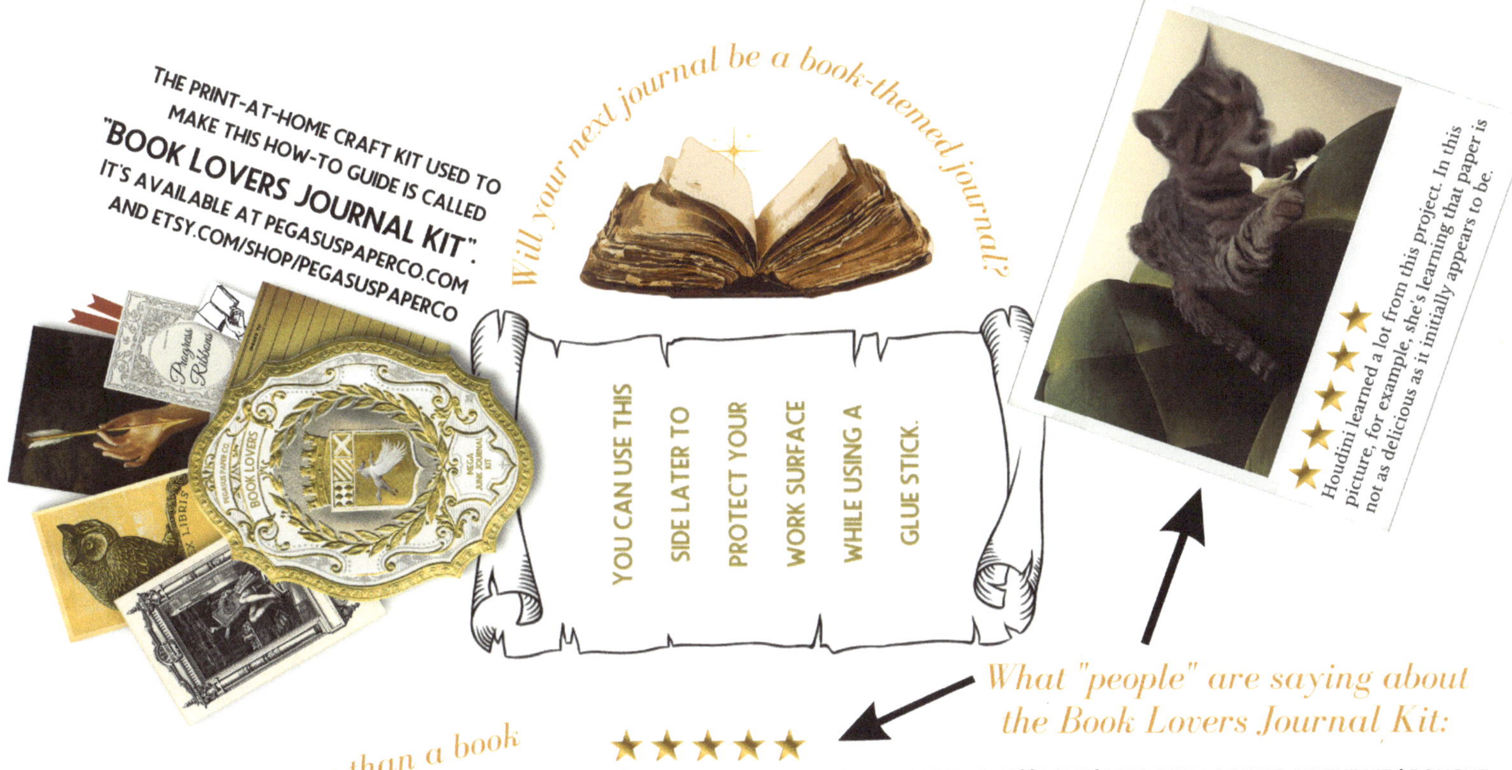

"The only thing better than a book is a book about books!"
-Sarah Zar

What "people" are saying about the Book Lovers Journal Kit:

★★★★★
"THANK YOU SO MUCH FOR MAKING THIS KIT! I LOVE I WAS JUST LOOKING AT THE KIT I BOUGHT AND I AM FLABBERGASTED AT THE QUALITY OF THE ITEMS! THERE ARE SO MANY GREAT FUSSY CUT IMAGES. ENVELOPES AND MORE! THE MARBLEIZED END PAPERS ARE SO COLORFUL! IT'S SO AMAZING. MY KIDS ARE ALL GOING TO LOVE THEIR GIFTS THIS YEAR. I HAVE A LOT OF BOOK READERS IN MY FAMILY AND THERE ARE PIECES AND PARTS FROM THE KIT THAT WILL BE WONDERFUL GIFTS." - MICHELLE

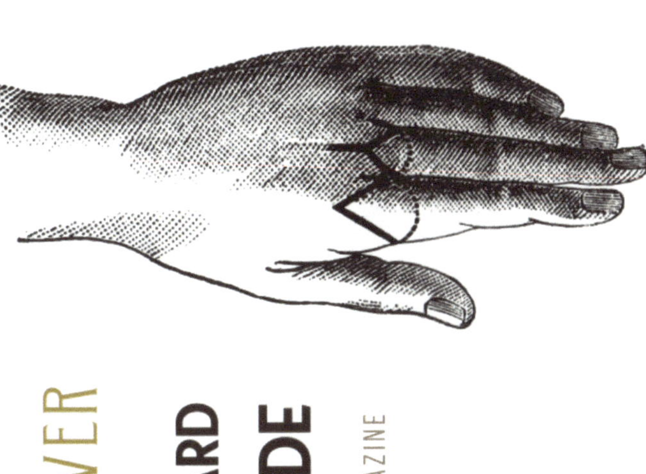

BOOK COVER
CARDBOARD SIZE GUIDE
JUNK JOURNAL MAGAZINE

1. FOLD THIS PAGE IN HALF ALONG THE LINE. (INSTRUCTIONS CONTINUE ON THE BACK.)

2. PLACE THIS SIDE OVER THE CARDBOARD YOU'LL USE FOR YOUR BOOK COVER. AND TRACE A LINE AROUND THE EDGE. THIS IS THE SIZE YOUR CARDBOARD SHOULD BE.

3. TRACE AND CUT OUT A FRONT AND BACK COVER. THESE COVERS SHOULD BE THE SAME SIZE AS YOUR PAGES.

Once the cover glue dries, fold your two marbled endpapers in half (each with the printed side facing in). *You can use the inside cover of this magazine.

Glue (or tape/glue stick) half of the endpaper to the inside of the cardboard cover of your book. Then use a glue stick to attach the other half of the marbled page to the first page of your book. Use a brayer or rolling pin to make sure it's firmly glued together and doesn't have air bubbles. This mighty marbled paper is what holds on the entire cover, so take extra care with it.

Wrap the remaining three edges from the front cover art over the marbled endpaper and use double-sided tape (or glue, or a glue stick) **to hold the flaps down.**

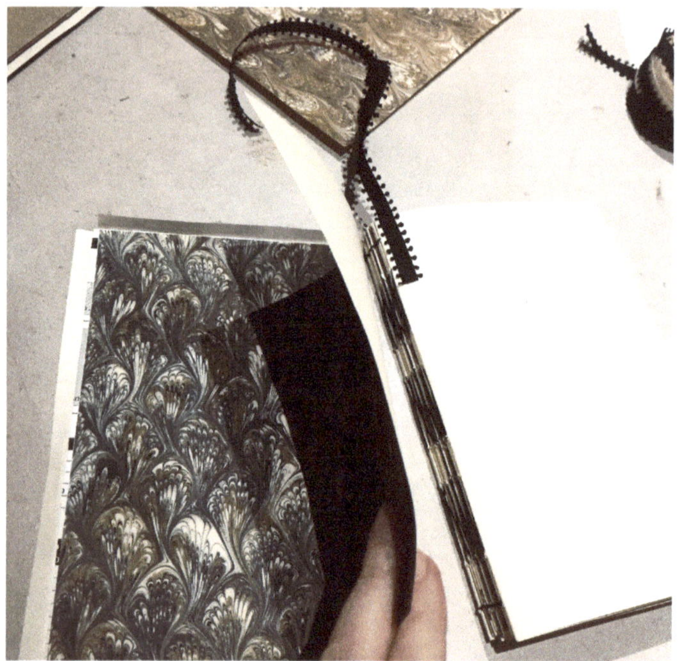

Do the same thing with the back cover.

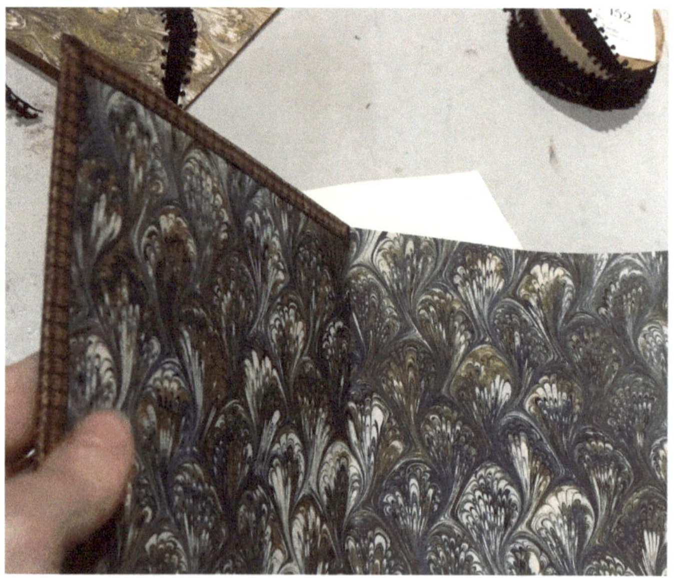

Gently clean off any excess glue, then press the book under something heavy for an hour. Not sure what to use? I'm guessing you like books? You can always put parchment paper on any potentially sticky surfaces to protect your books. Keep stacking them on until it looks like they're pressing down firmly, helping to lock the glue in as it dries.

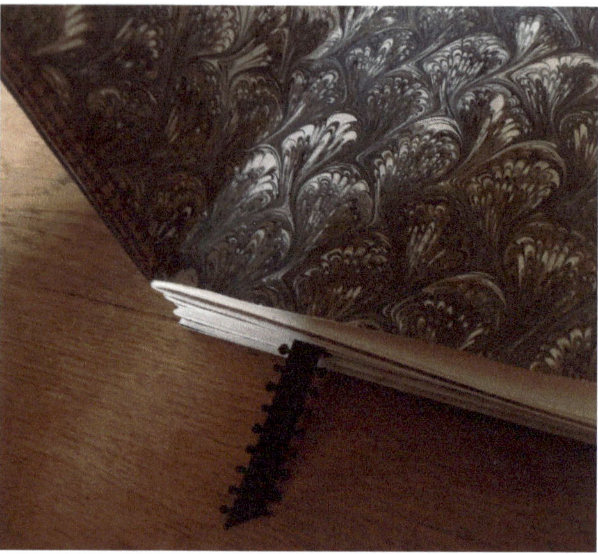

Shall we stop here for a cup of tea, or keep going?

☐ Oo, tea sounds good! Or something else....

☐ There is no stopping me! I am a force of nature!

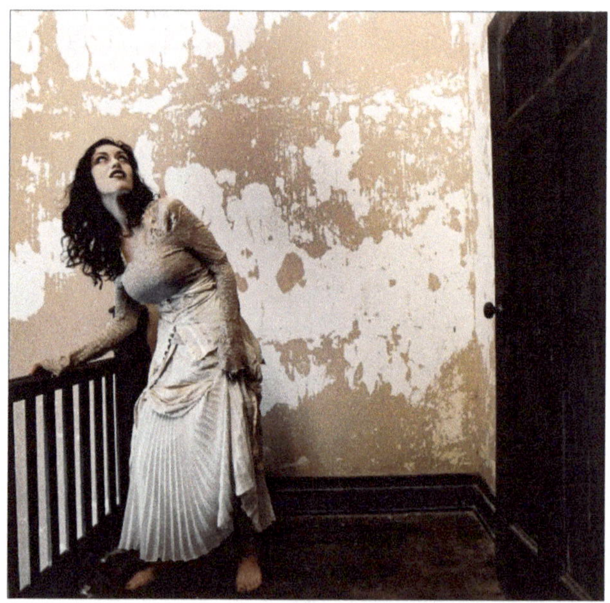

Photograph by Leif Zurmuhlen

Sarah Zar here, just popping in to say that if you've crafted your way here, you're doing so well! And you're almost at my favorite part! If you have any questions or need help, you can post them in the private group at **facebook.com/JunkJournalMagazine/groups**

FRONT COVER

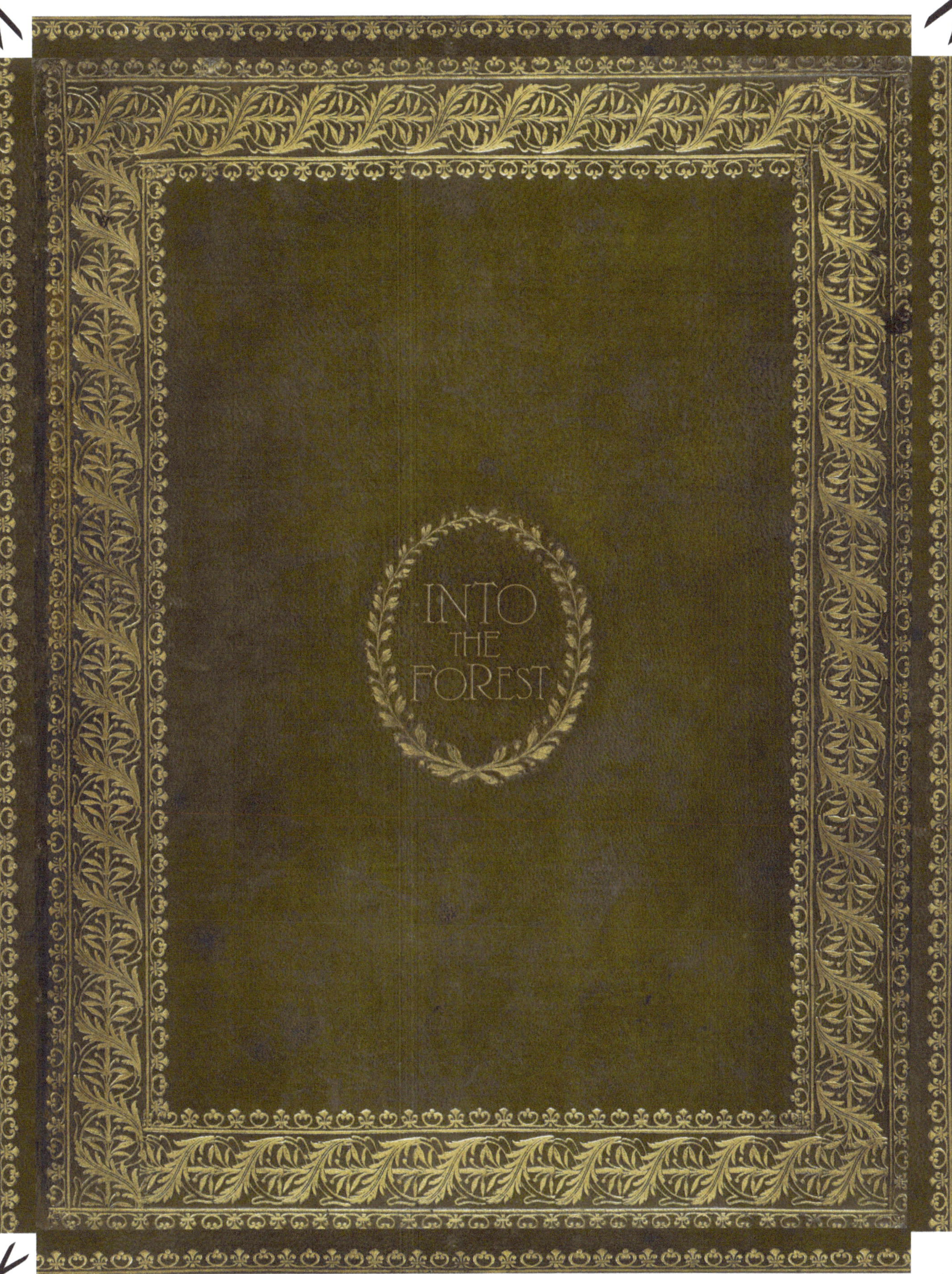

INTO
THE
FOREST

THE GOLDEN EDGING CAN BE WRAPPED AROUND A PIECE OF CARDBOARD, AND GLUED DOWN TO CREATE A COVER FOR YOUR JOURNAL. CEREAL BOX CARDBOARD WORKS VERY WELL. YOU CAN ALSO UP-CYCLE CARDBOARD DELIVERY BOXES INTO A JOURNAL COVER.

• TIP: AFTER GLUING PAPER TO CARDBOARD, PRESS FIRMLY USE A ROLLING PIN OR BRAYER. PUT A HEAVY WEIGHT ON TOP SO IT DRIES FLAT.

Alternate Cover Option

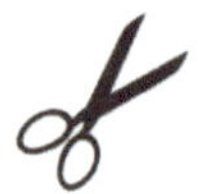

The golden edging can be wrapped around a piece of cardboard, and glued down to create a cover for your journal. Cereal box cardboard works very well. You can also up-cycle cardboard delivery boxes into a journal cover.

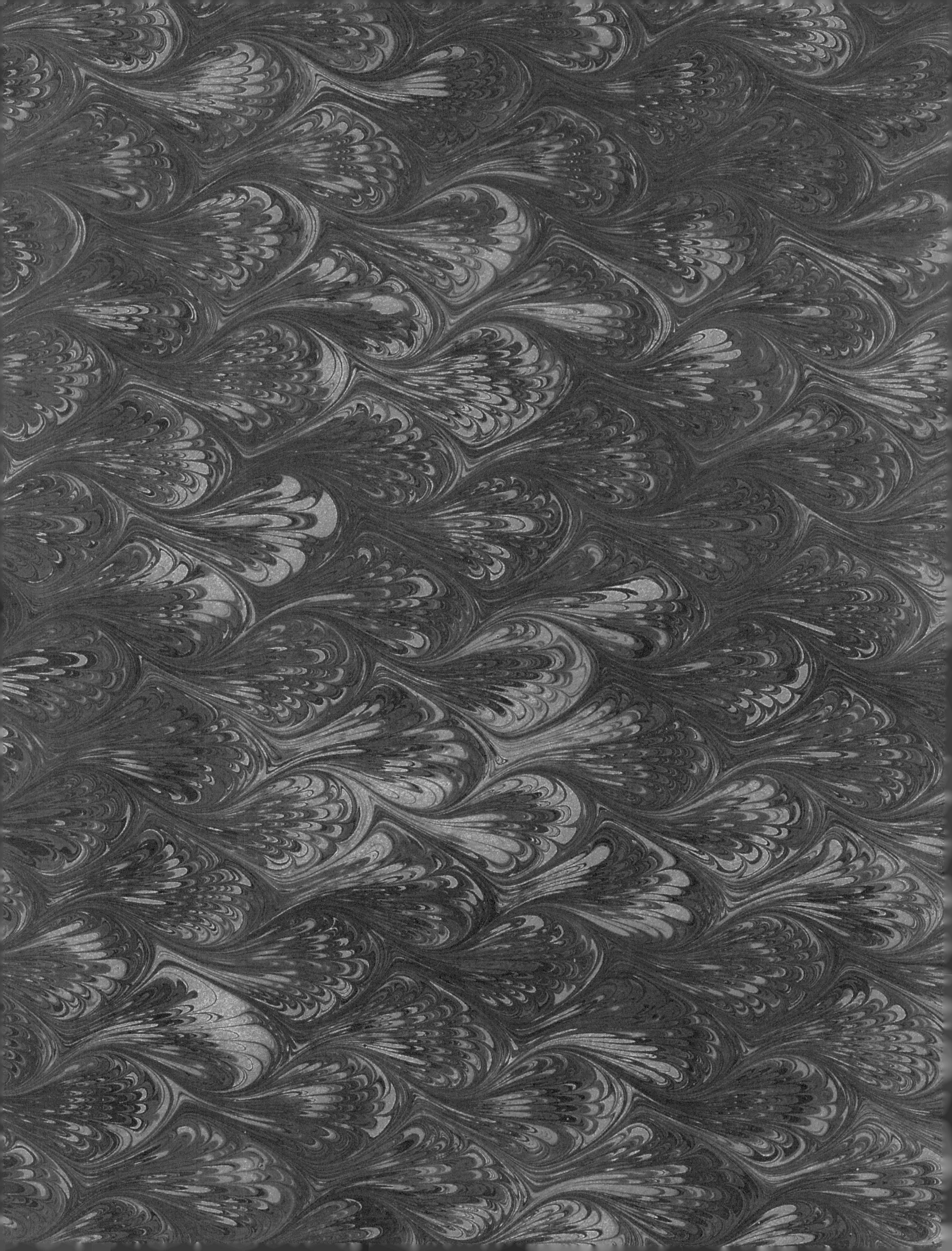

- ONCE YOU GET ALL YOUR FOLDED PAPERS STACKED UP, YOU'LL BE ABLE TO SEE HOW WIDE TO MAKE THE CARDBOARD SPINE OF YOUR BOOK.
- I LIKE TO LEAVE EXTRA SPACE SO I CAN ADD LOTS OF EPHEMERA TO THE PAGES ONCE IT'S ASSEMBLED.
- CUT THE CARDBOARD FIRST, THEN WRAP THIS PAPER AROUND IT AND GLUE IT DOWN, PRESSING FIRMLY. IF IT DOESN'T COMPLETELY COVER THE INSIDE OF THE SPINE, YOU CAN USE OTHER PAPER SCRAPS SO THE CARDBOARD WON'T SHOW THROUGH IN YOUR FINISHED JOURNAL.

*If you plan to use this spine paper, please have a glance at Step 5 on the back first.

Step 5

ADORNMENT & EPHEMERA

Now that the glue is dry, and your book is pressed nicely into shape, you're ready to start collaging in ephemera and writing on the pages! I like to cut out all the pictures, assemble any mini- projects and add-on elements I have, and gather any special little scraps from my own collection that would go well with the theme of my journal. **Then you can move things around and see what looks good together, and generally have a marvelous time seeking out beautiful visual harmonies. When something *'clicks'* for you, attach it right there!**

Junk Journal Magazine already includes on-page prompts for assembling the complex decorative ephemera and folding envelopes, so I'll just post some photos of the process here, along with a few tips. Remember, there are no rules! You can personalize your journal in any way that pleases you. You can color in ephemera, add ribbons, tape/glue/sew things onto the pages, add extra pockets and postcards, hide little surprises in envelopes, and so on.

I'd love to see what you create with these pages! You can upload photo reviews online, or tag #junkjournalmagazine @JUNKJOURNALMAGAZINE to show off your journal!

- **ARTIST-DESIGNED KITS:** If you're reading this in JUNK JOURNAL MAGAZINE, or in one of the PEGASUS PAPER CO. mega journal kits, those come with a curated selection of gorgeous ephemera to match your project!
- **MIX & MATCH DIGITAL DOWNLOADS:** If you have access to a printer, you can find a wonderful selection of printable ephemera in the FREE LIBRARY at pegasuspaperco.com There are also a number of very detailed papers and journal kits available in the shop for digital download.
- **AROUND THE HOUSE:** Any loose bit is fair game!

When I started making junk journals, suddenly, I looked at every scrap and color as a resource for making wonderful, bookish treasures! I hope that the process of creating this project helps you look at the world in a new way too. You and the world are full of treasures, and I believe that the more you create, the richer those treasures become. The richer your sight becomes. The richer your days can feel, and the more you have to share with others. Thank you for joining me, and...

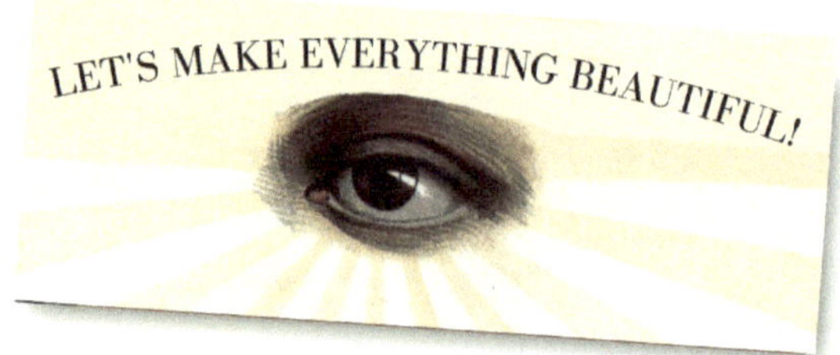

Until soon,
Sarah

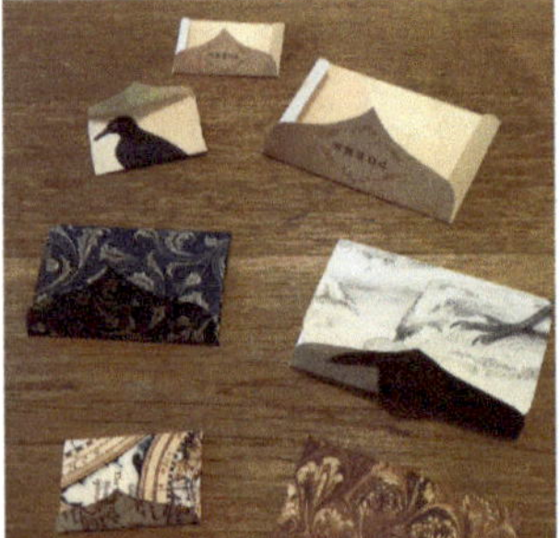

You can trace the envelope from this project and make more out of scrap papers, magazine pages, or old book pages.

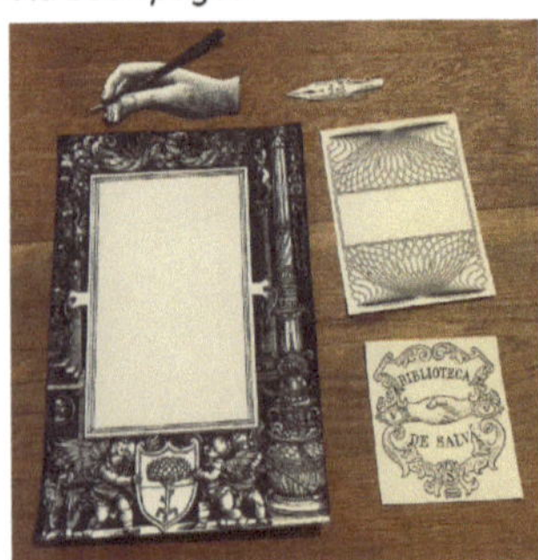

In the world of junk journaling, a piece of paper with space for you to write is called a JOURNAL CARD. Hide some in your book!

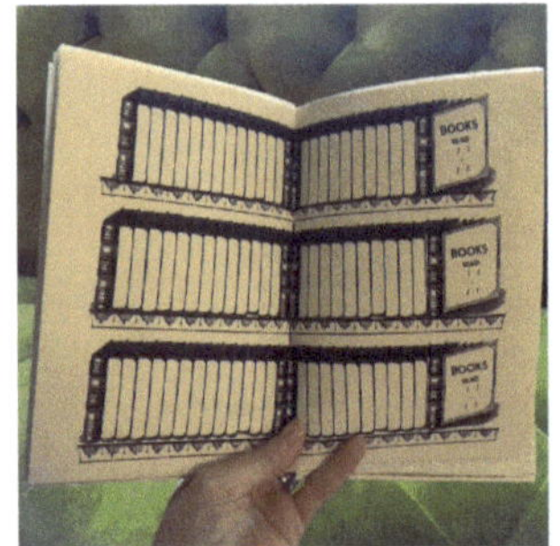

I'll write the names of books along the spine of each book, as I finish it. I've always wanted a record of what I've read.

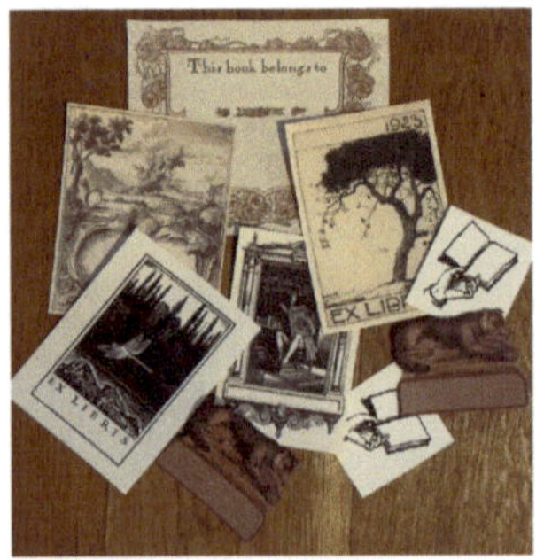

I like to cut everything out, then play with my craft supplies and find interesting ways to collage and attach things to pages.

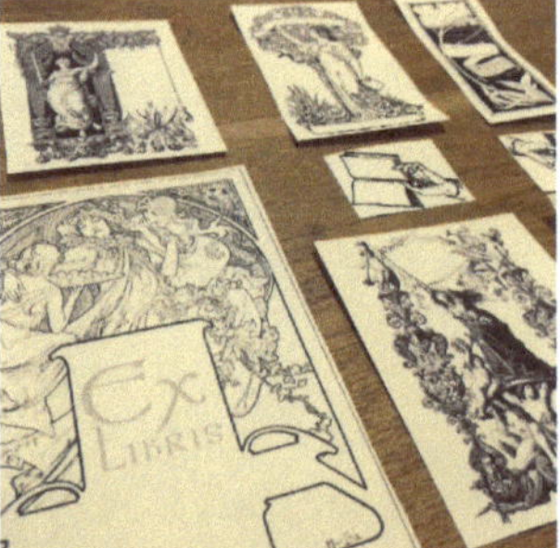

Remember, ephemera can be colored in, or inked around the edges, brushed with gold powder, collaged into pages, and more!

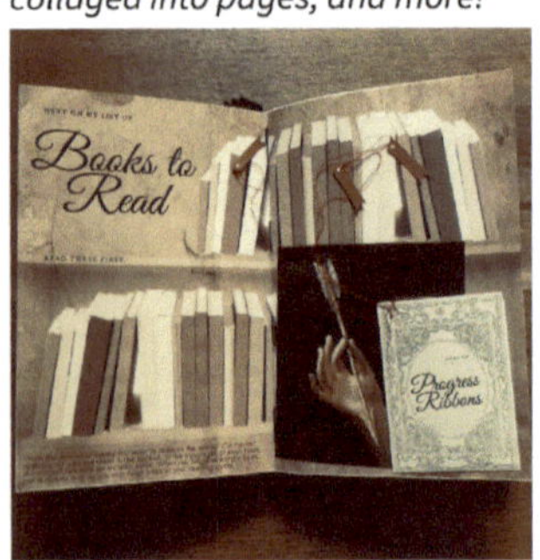

Sewing into the paper also adds an extra bit of interest and texture! What other treasures could be sewn on? Sequins? Lace?

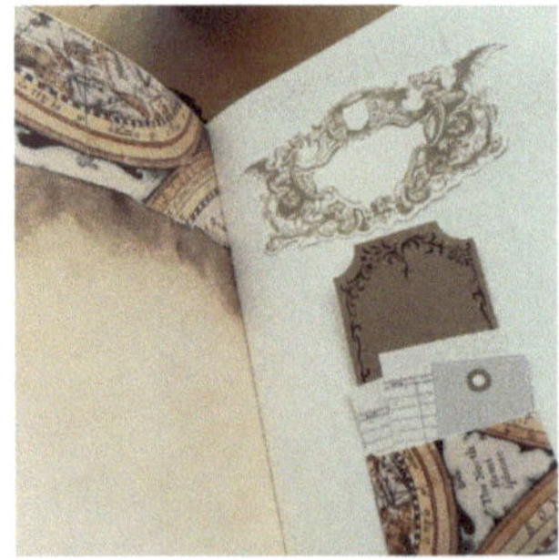

Mini-envelopes/pockets/tucks can hold extra tags... Or stickers, bookmarks, and stamps!

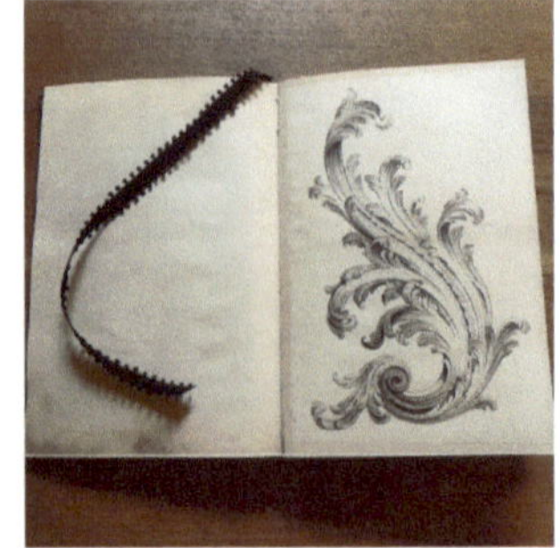

Use your journal to draw, write, collage, collect memories, plan, or dream... it will expand as you do!

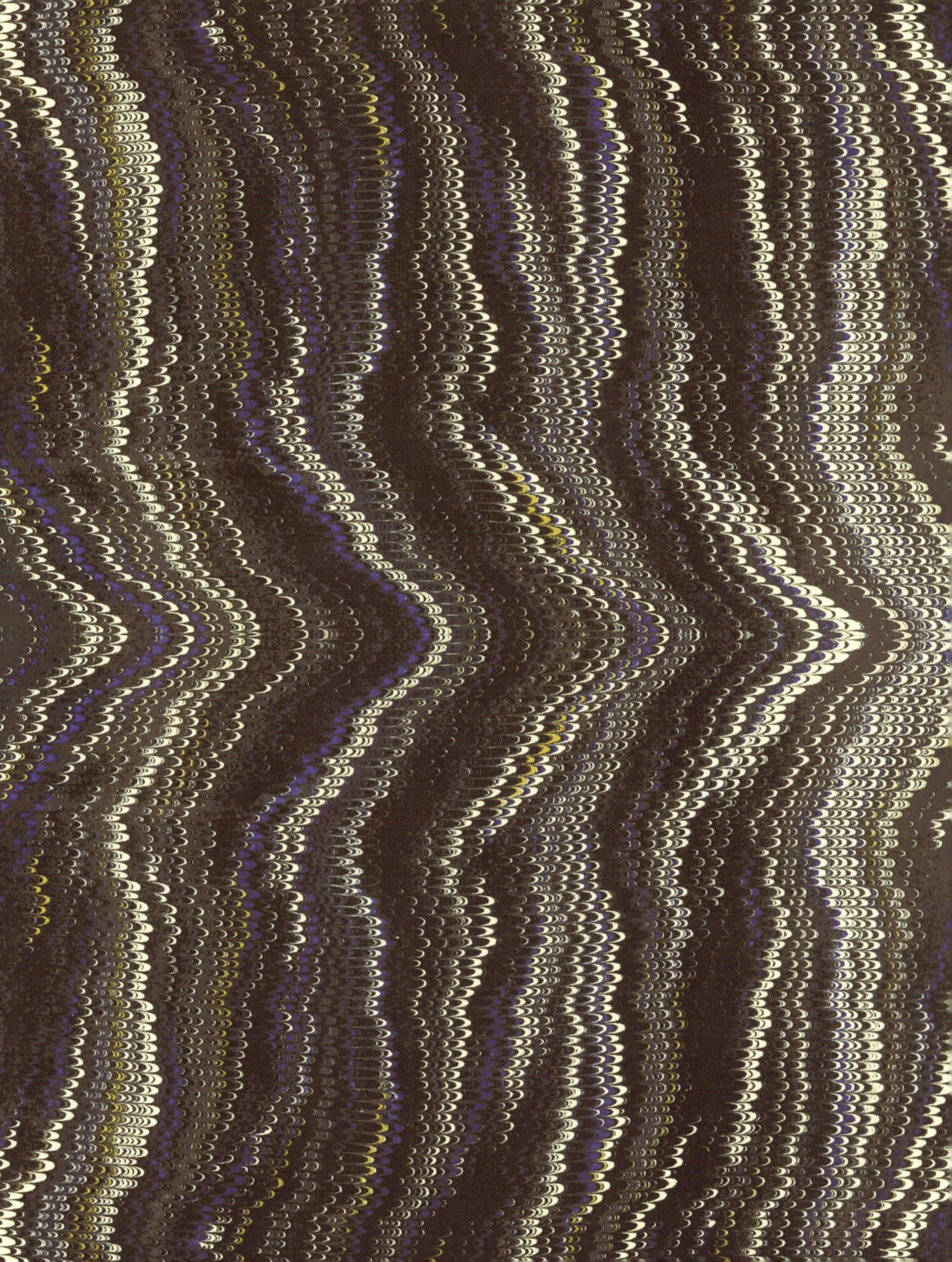

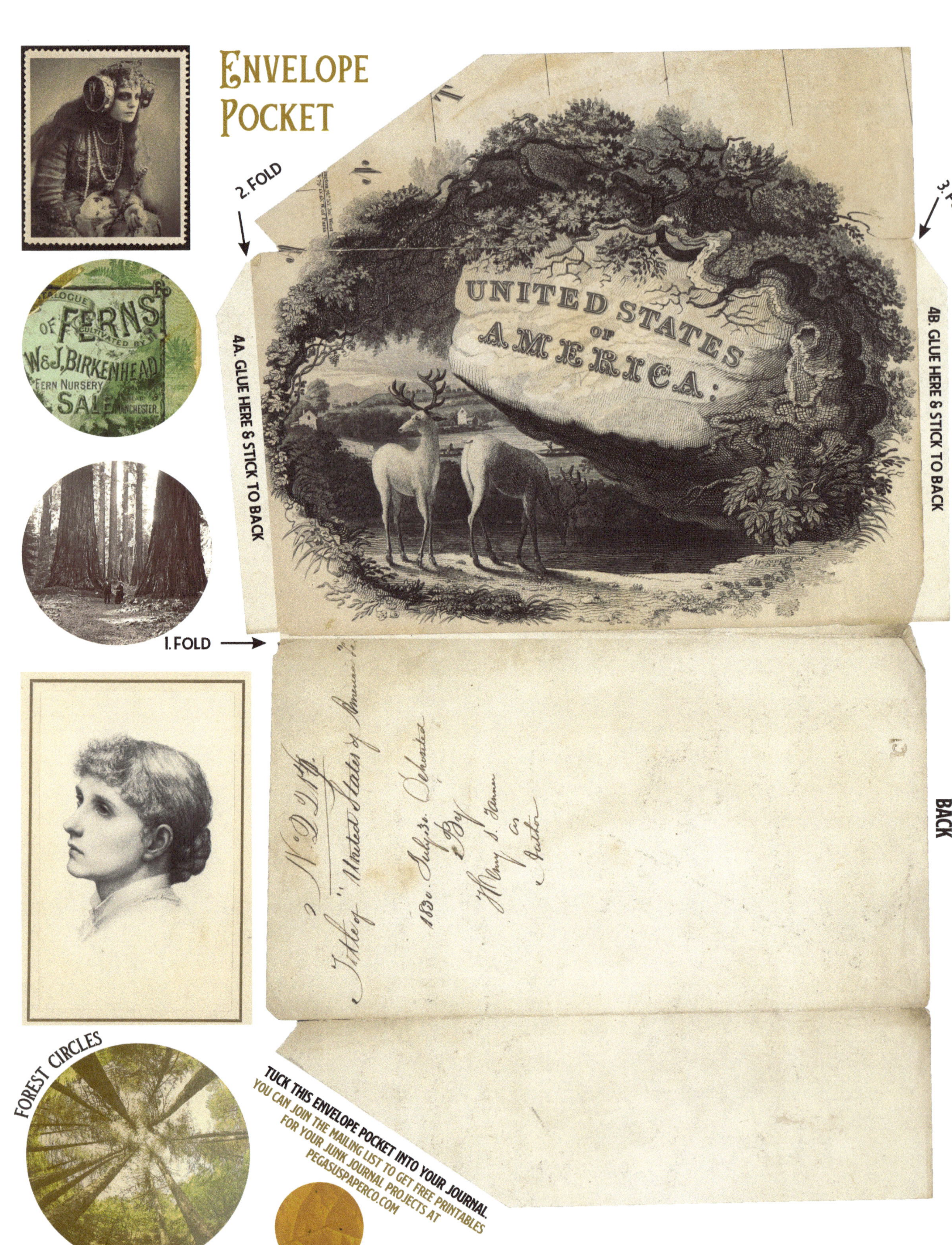

ENVELOPE POCKET
2. FOLD
3. FOLD
4A. GLUE HERE & STICK TO BACK
4B. GLUE HERE & STICK TO BACK
1. FOLD
BACK
UNITED STATES OF AMERICA.
CATALOGUE OF FERNS CULTIVATED BY W & J BIRKENHEAD FERN NURSERY SALE MANCHESTER.
FOREST CIRCLES
TUCK THIS ENVELOPE POCKET INTO YOUR JOURNAL. YOU CAN JOIN THE MAILING LIST TO GET FREE PRINTABLES FOR YOUR JUNK JOURNAL PROJECTS AT PEGASUSPAPERCO.COM

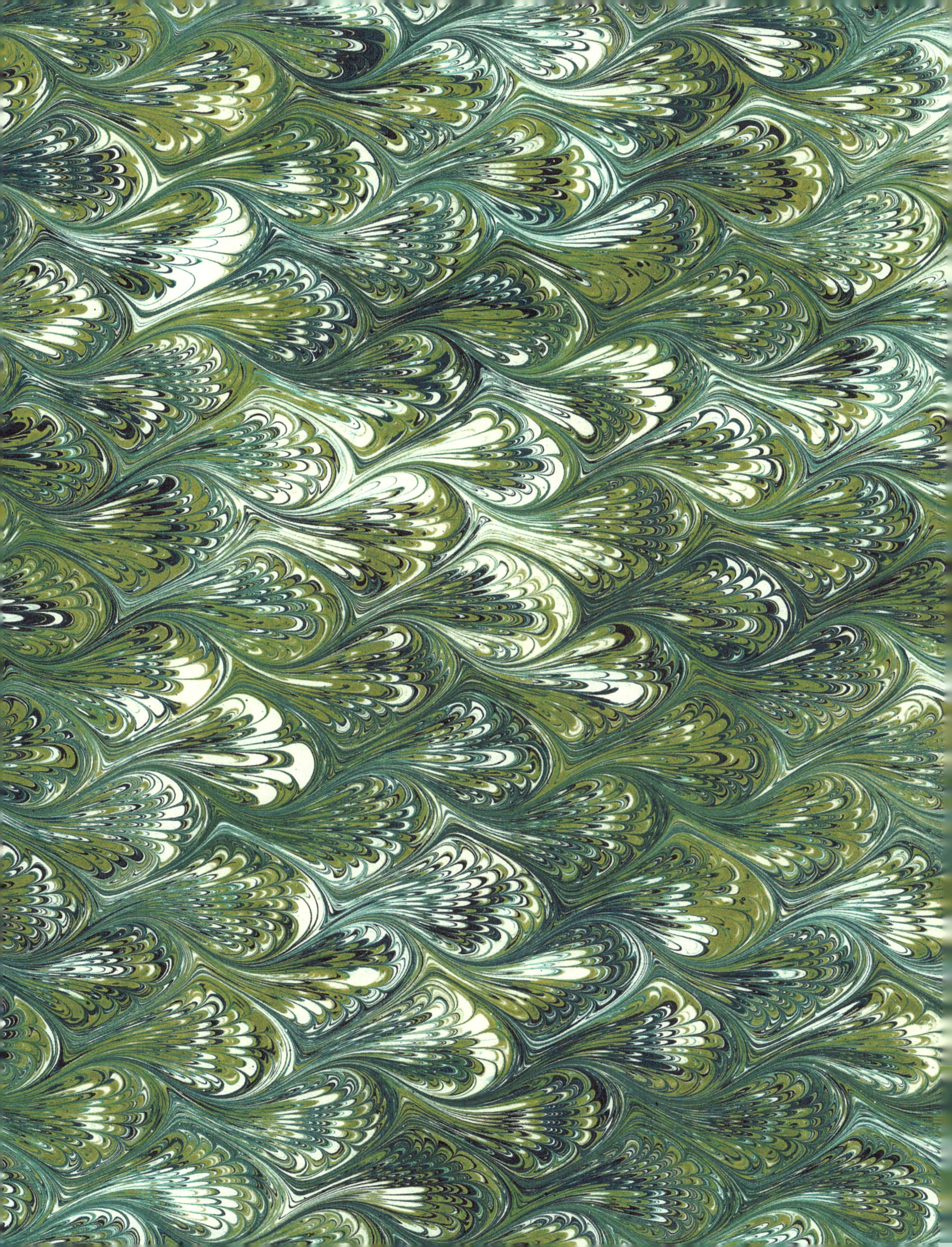

POCKETS
FOLD THE EDGES AND GLUE THEM TO ANY PAGE TO CREATE A LITTLE POCKET

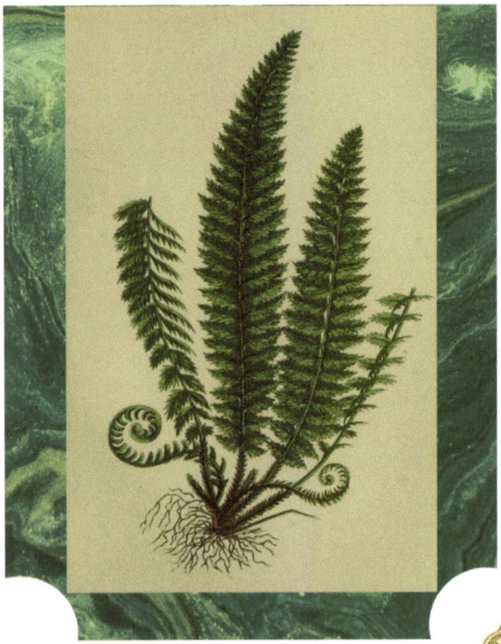

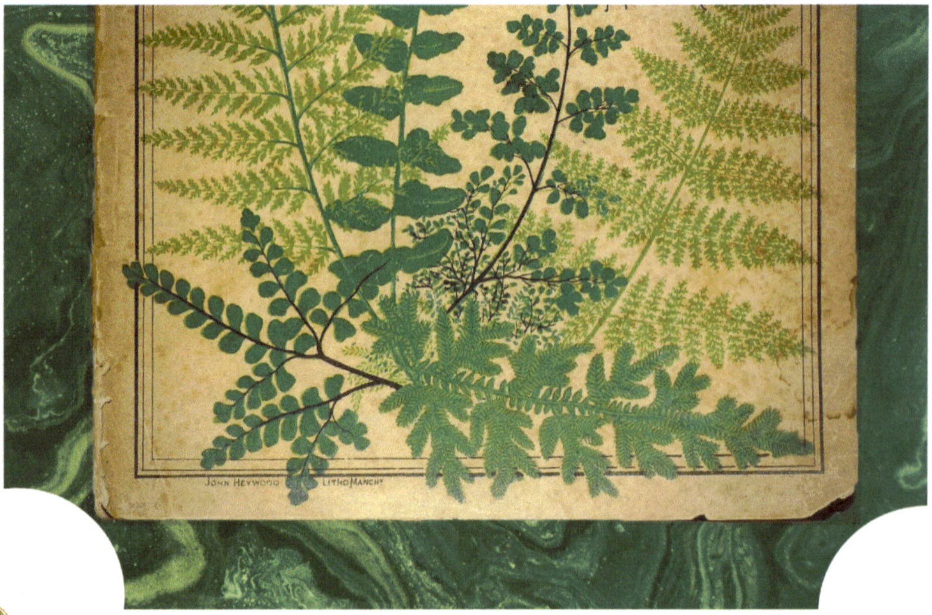

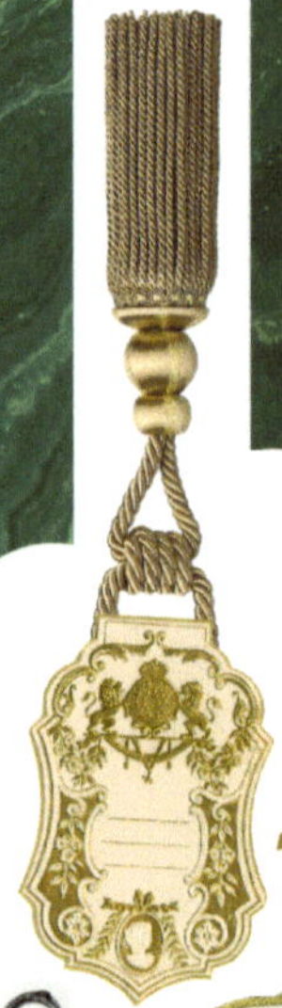

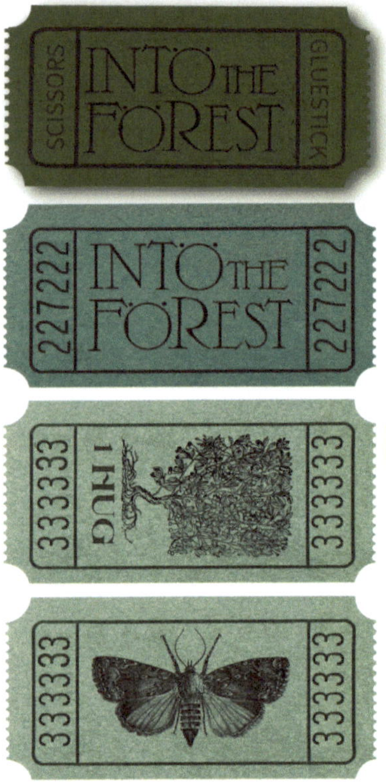

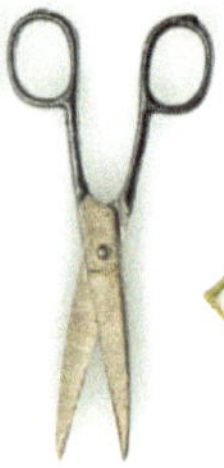

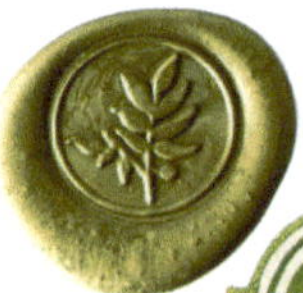

TAGS
FOLD IN HALF. AROUND A STRING OR TASSEL AND GLUE.

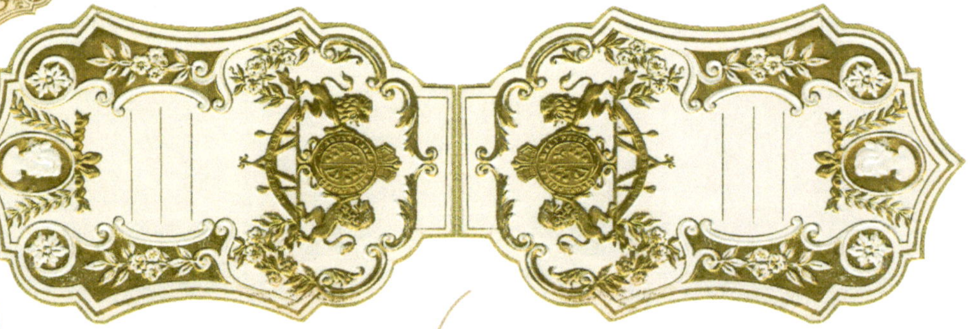

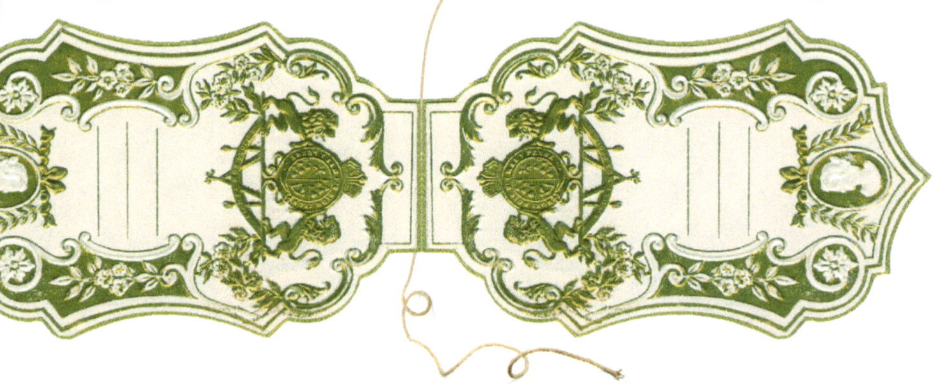

INDEX TABS
FOLD THE INDEX TABS (BELOW) AROUND THE EDGE OF ANY PAGE TO CREATE A LABELED SECTION MARKER.

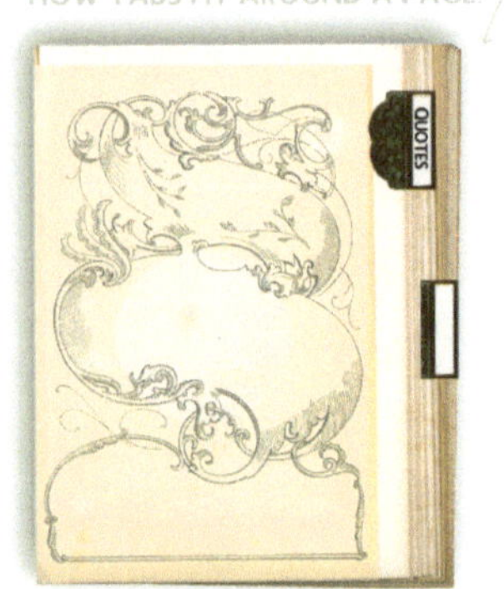

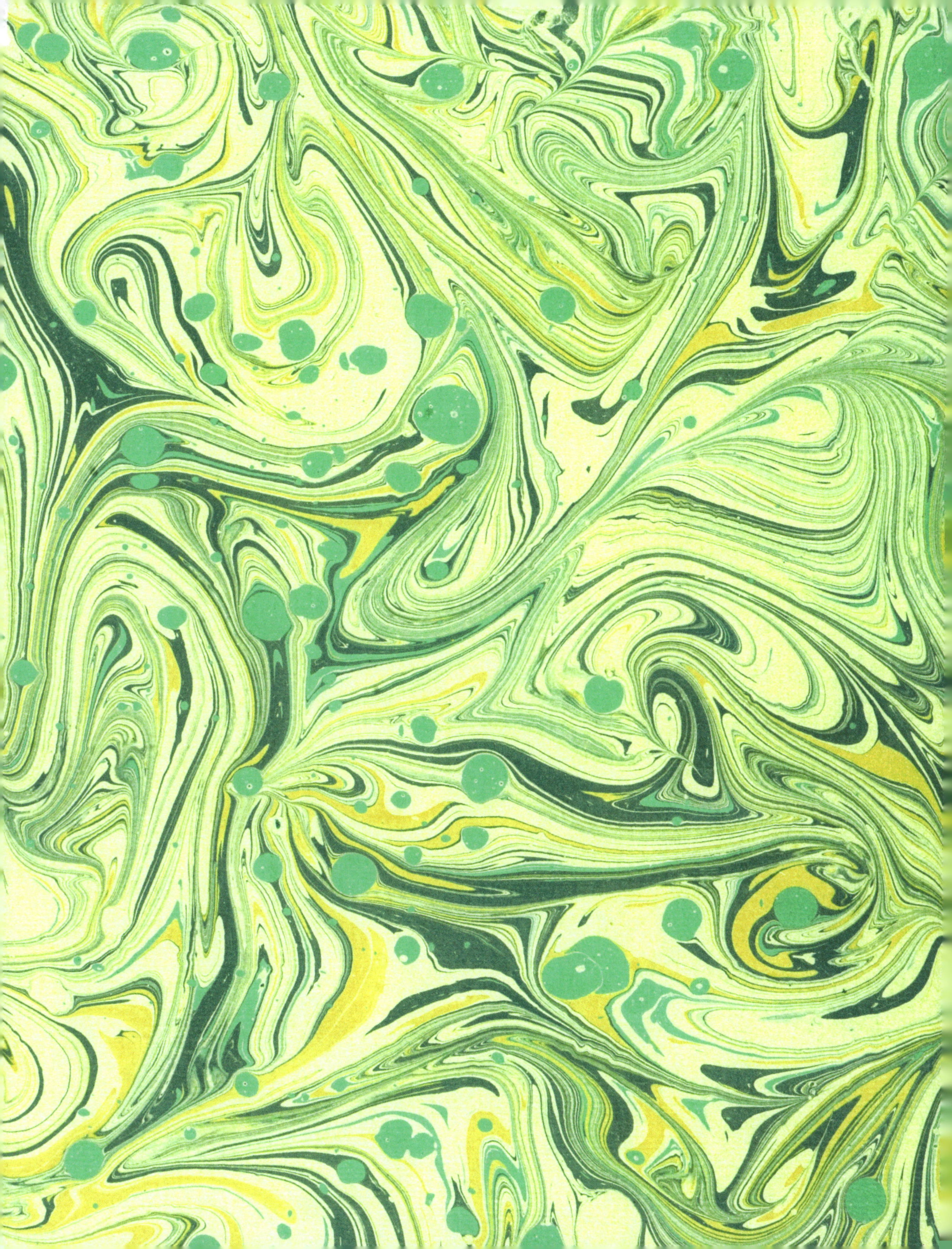

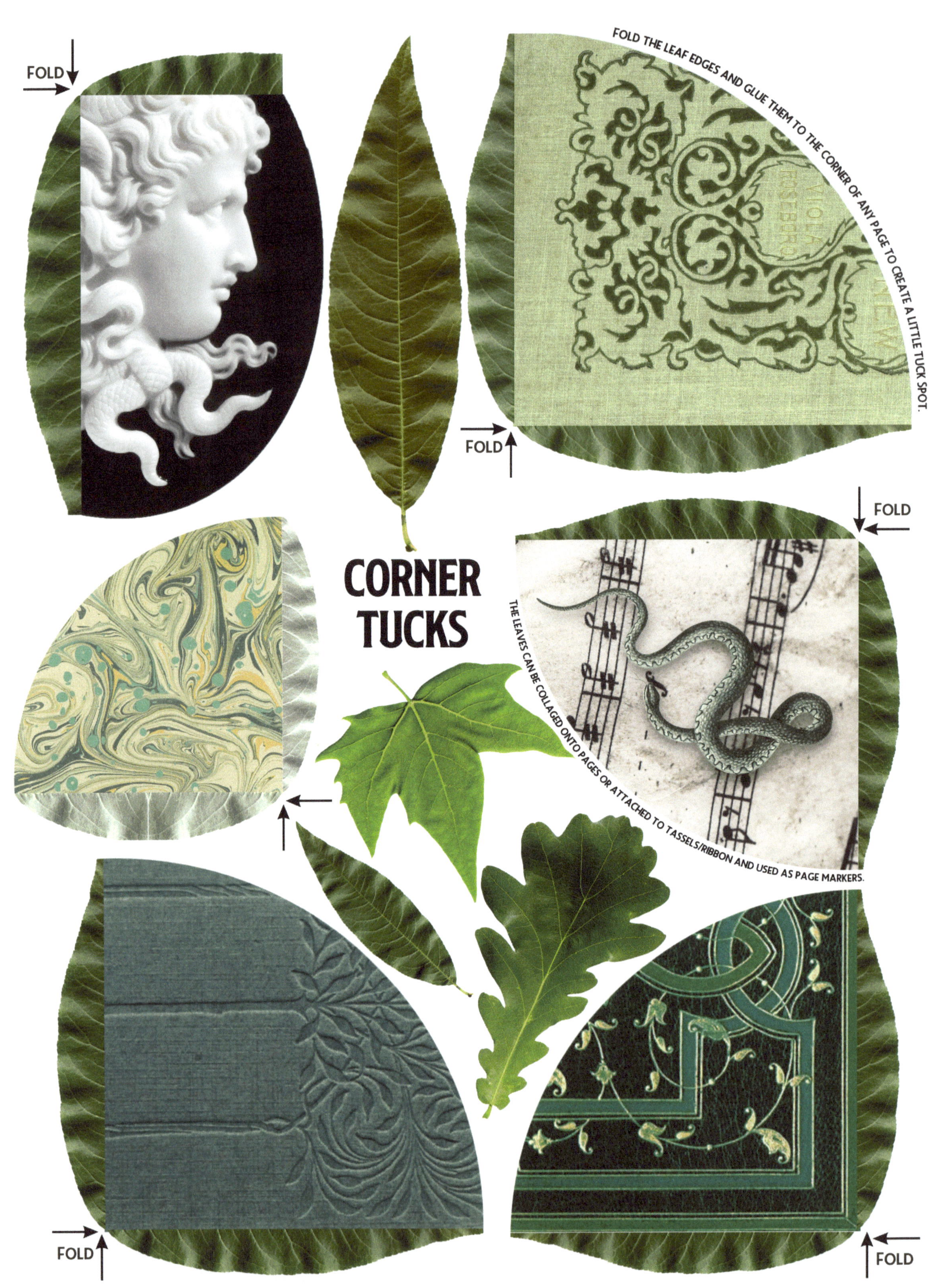

FOLD
FOLD THE LEAF EDGES AND GLUE THEM TO THE CORNER OF ANY PAGE TO CREATE A LITTLE TUCK SPOT.
FOLD
FOLD
CORNER TUCKS
THE LEAVES CAN BE COLLAGED ONTO PAGES OR ATTACHED TO TASSELS/RIBBON AND USED AS PAGE MARKERS.
FOLD
FOLD

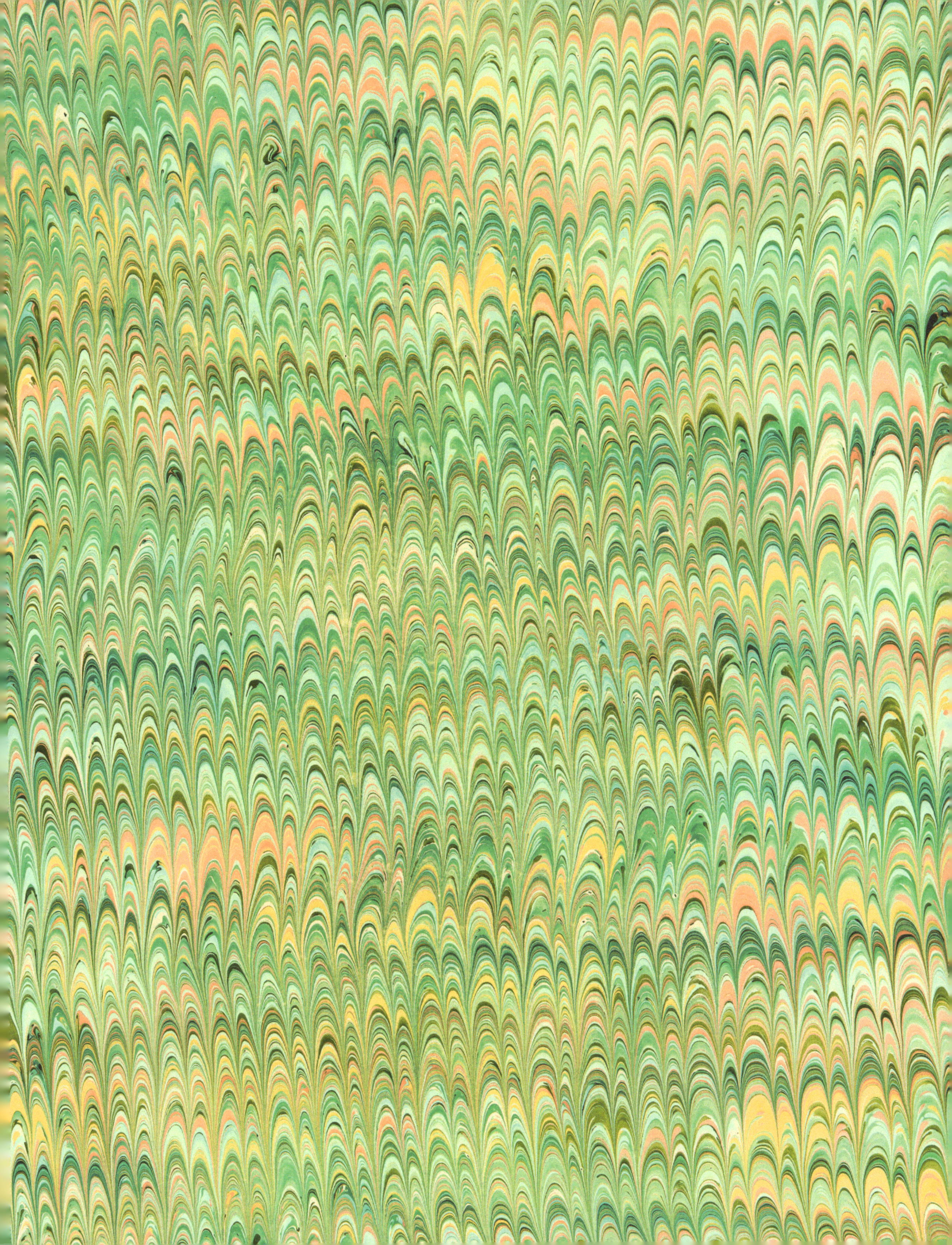

JOURNAL CARD TO WRITE ON.   POCKET FOLD THE EDGES AND GLUE THEM TO ANY PAGE.

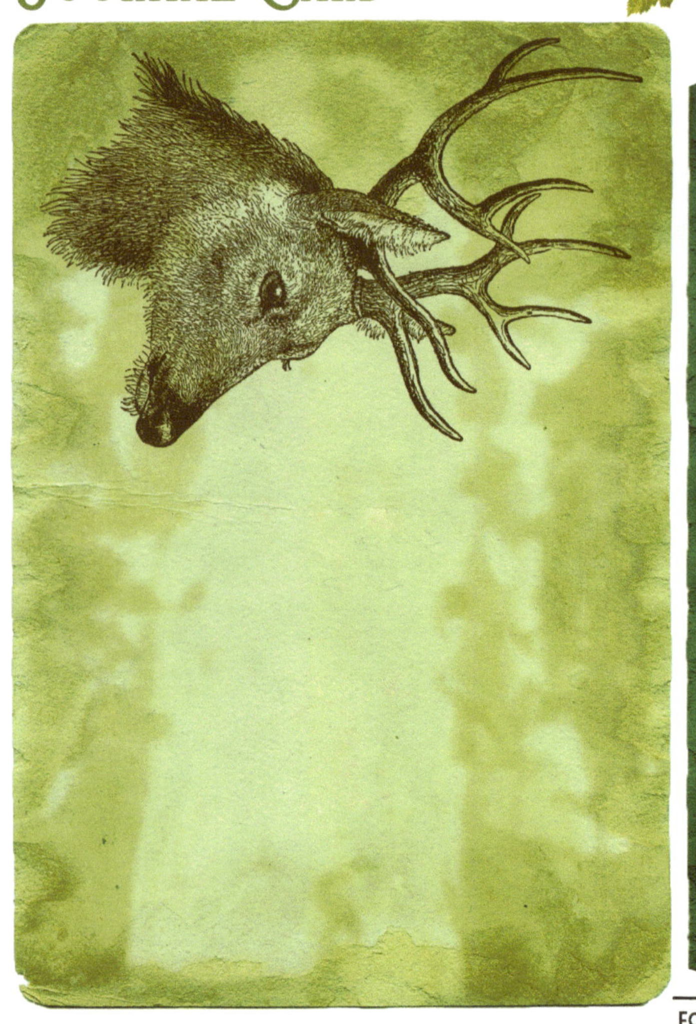

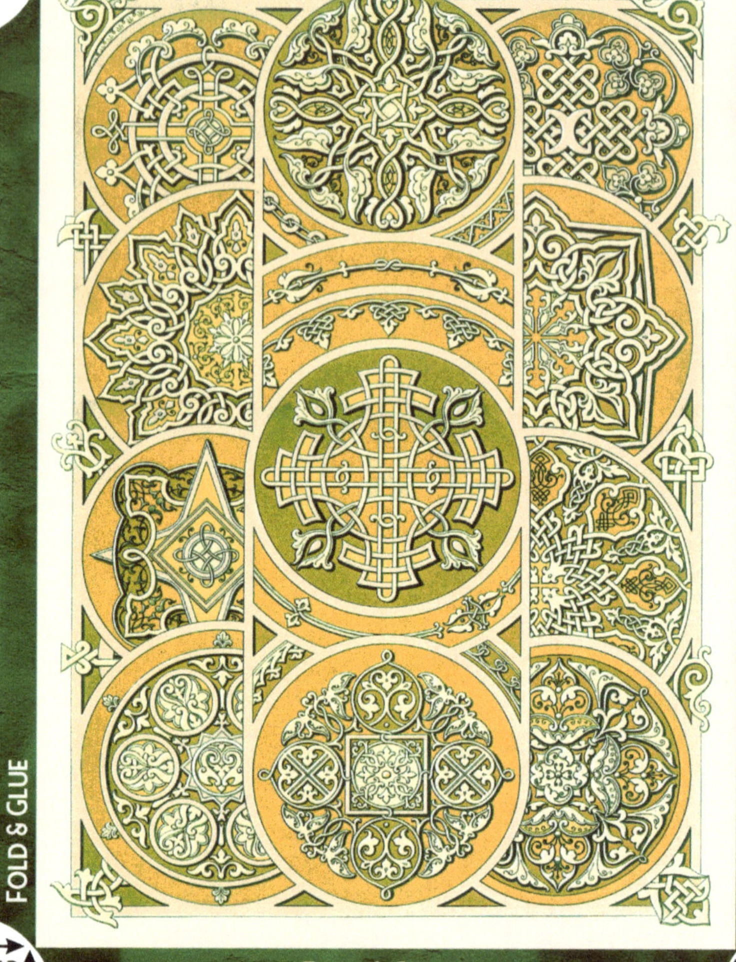

FOLD & GLUE
FOLD & GLUE
FOLD
FOLD & GLUE
FOLD

BELLY BAND
GLUE THE SHORT EDGES TO A PAGE AND TUCK TAGS OR EPHEMERA INTO THIS BAND.

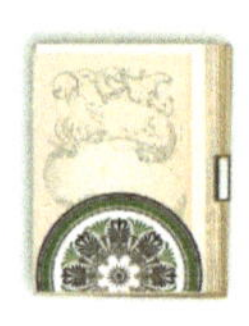

TUCK SPOT

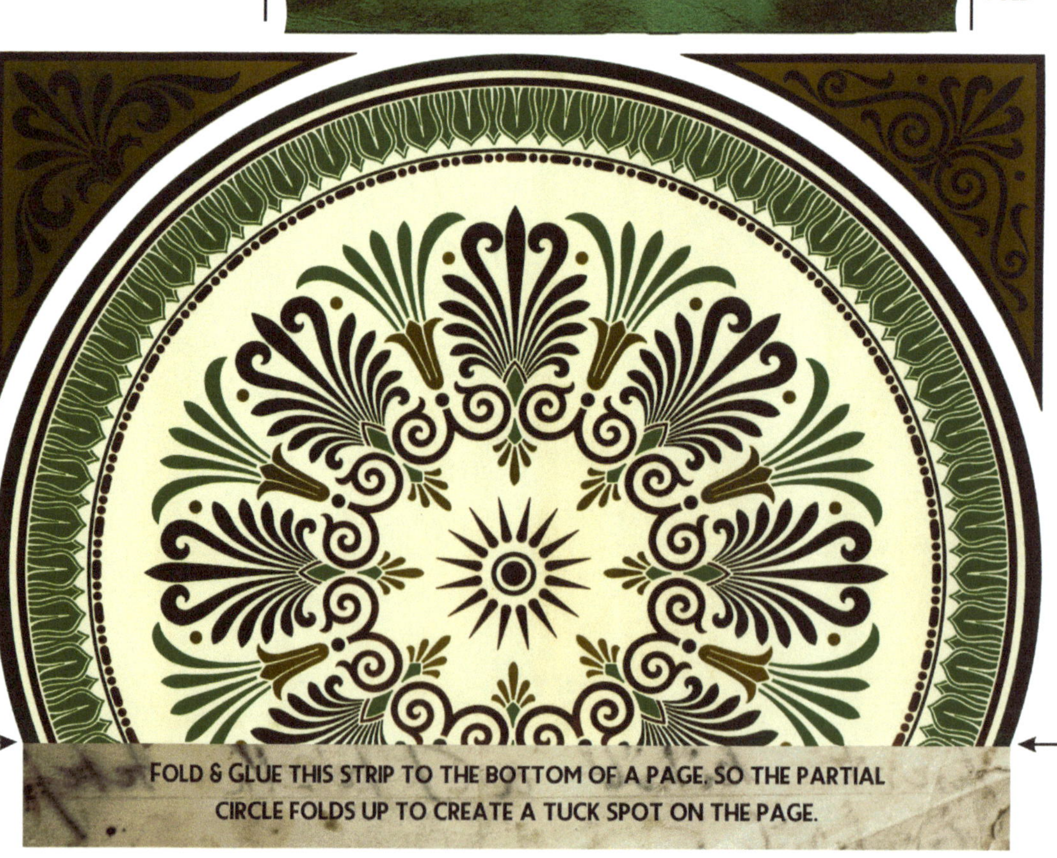

FOLD & GLUE THIS STRIP TO THE BOTTOM OF A PAGE, SO THE PARTIAL
CIRCLE FOLDS UP TO CREATE A TUCK SPOT ON THE PAGE.

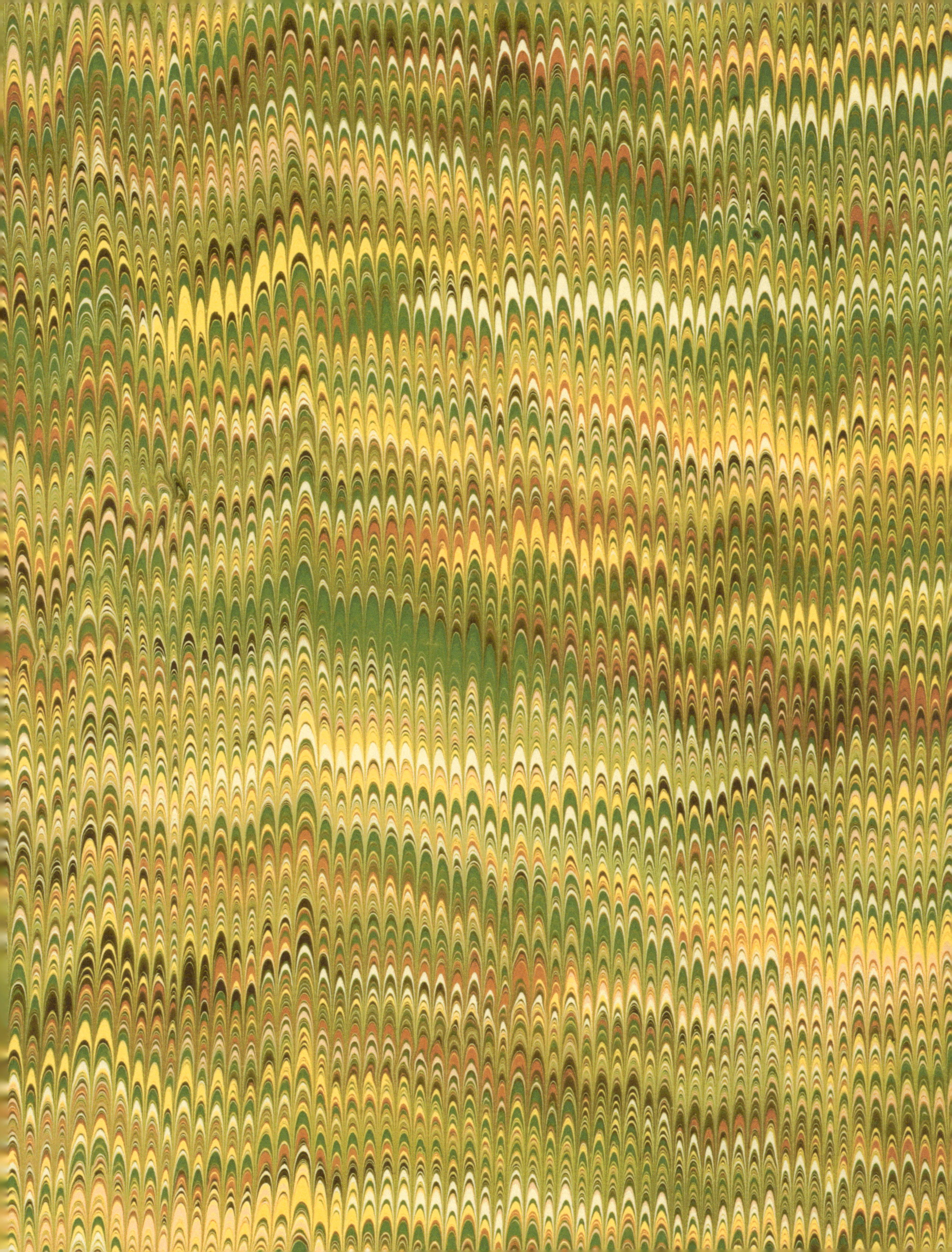

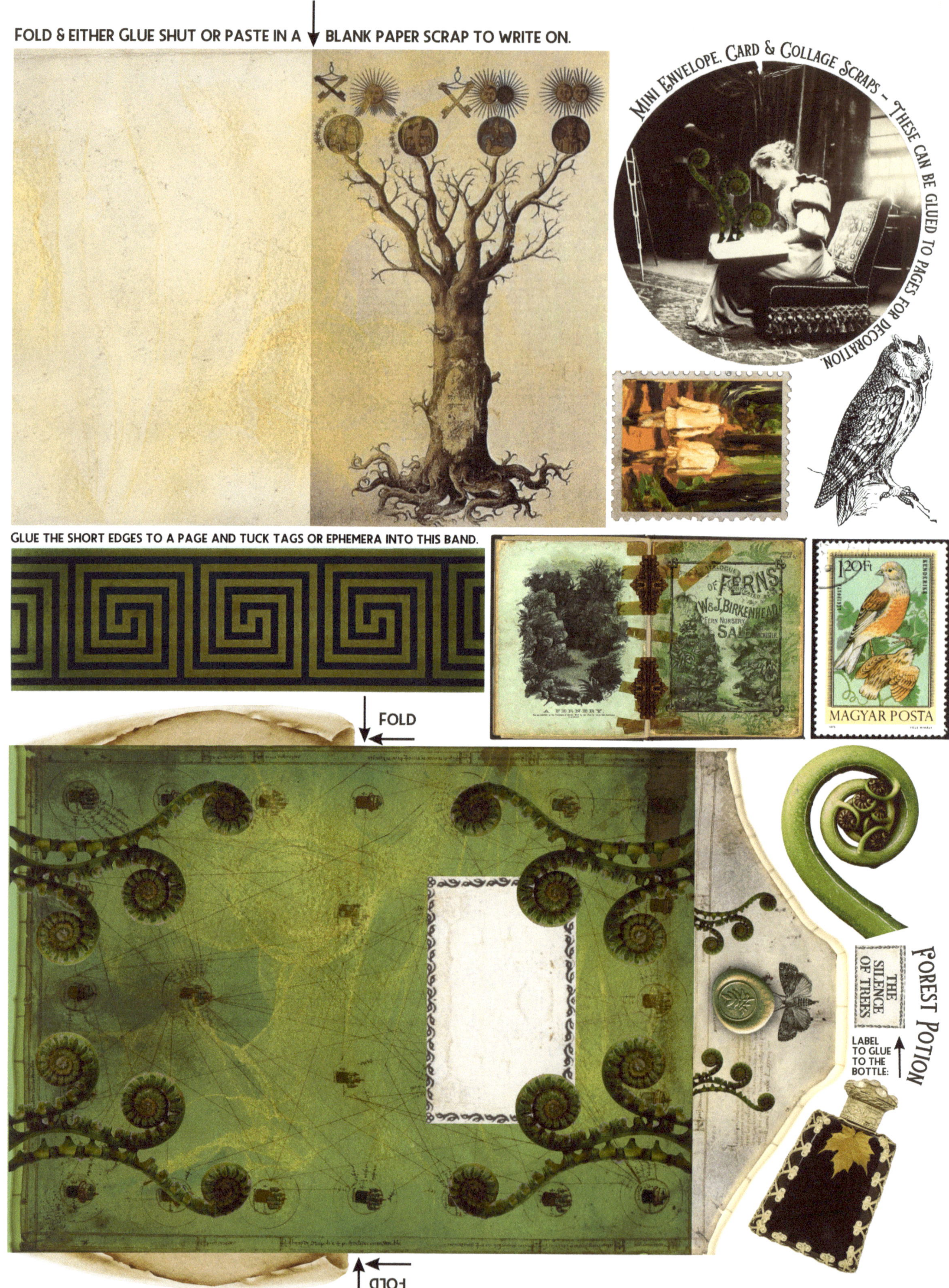

FOLD & EITHER GLUE SHUT OR PASTE IN A   BLANK PAPER SCRAP TO WRITE ON.
MINI ENVELOPE, CARD & COLLAGE SCRAPS — THESE CAN BE GLUED TO PAGES FOR DECORATION.
GLUE THE SHORT EDGES TO A PAGE AND TUCK TAGS OR EPHEMERA INTO THIS BAND.
FOLD
FOLD
CATALOGUE OF FERNS
W & J. BIRKENHEAD
FERN NURSERY
SALE
A FERNERY
1.20 Ft
MAGYAR POSTA
FOREST POTION
THE SILENCE OF TREES
LABEL TO GLUE TO THE BOTTLE:

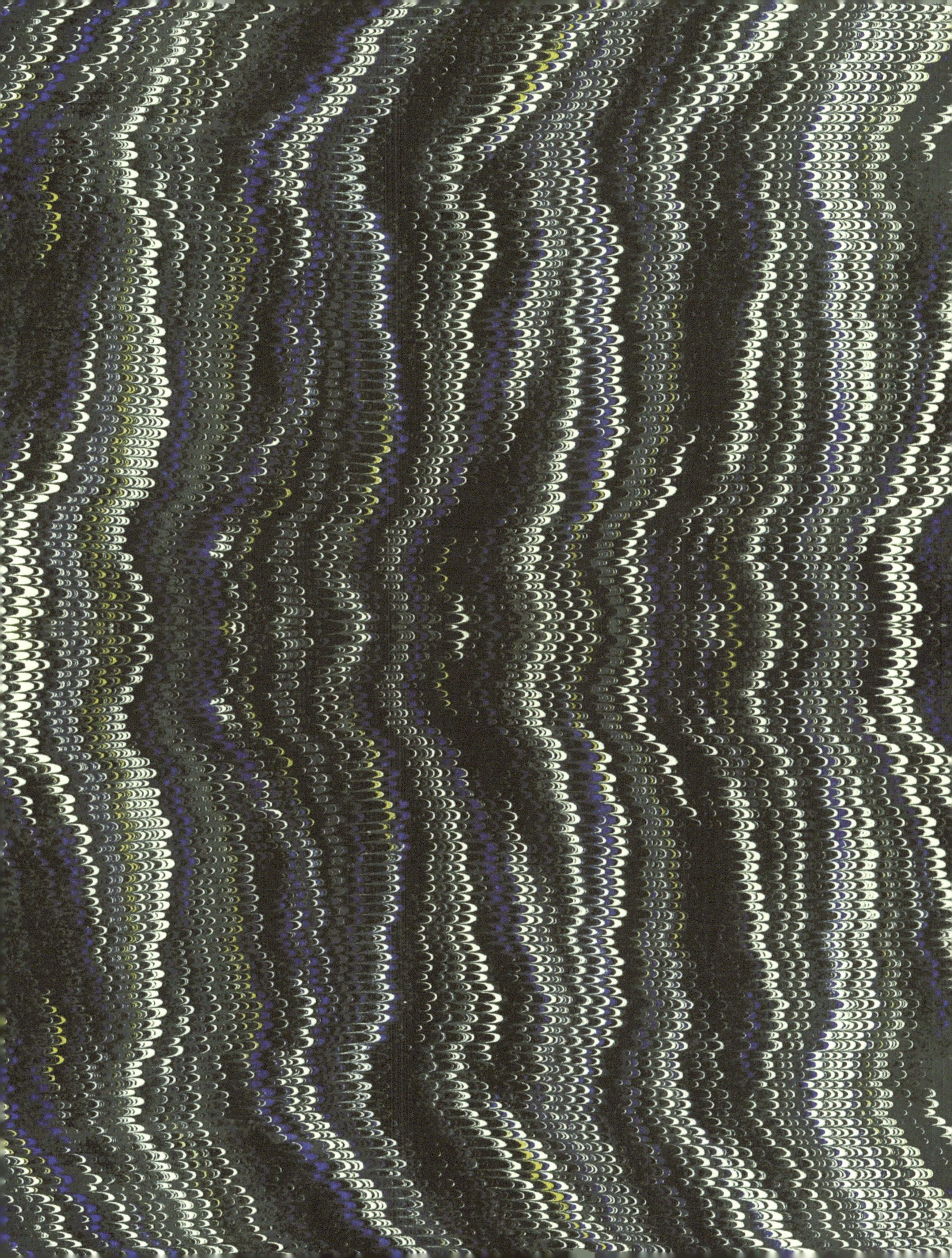

"Whoever has learned how to listen to trees no longer wants to be a tree. He wants to be nothing except what he is. That is home. That is happiness."

- Herman Hesse

"What lies behind us and what lies ahead of us are tiny matters compared to what lies within us."

- Henry David Thoreau

"Between every two pines is a doorway to a new world."

- John Muir

"The creation of a thousand forests is in one acorn."

- Ralph Waldo Emerson

"One touch of nature makes the whole world kin."

- William Shakespeare

"The clearest way into the Universe is through a forest wilderness."

- John Muir

"Forests are the lungs of our land, purifying the air and giving fresh strength to our people."

- Franklin D. Roosevelt

"Trees are poems that the earth writes upon the sky."

- Kahlil Gibran

"In a forest of a hundred thousand trees, no two leaves are alike. And no two journeys along the same path are alike."

- Paulo Coelho

"You know me, I think there ought to be a big old tree right there. And let's give him a friend. Everybody needs a friend."

- Bob Ross

"In all things of nature, there is something of the marvelous…"

- Aristotle

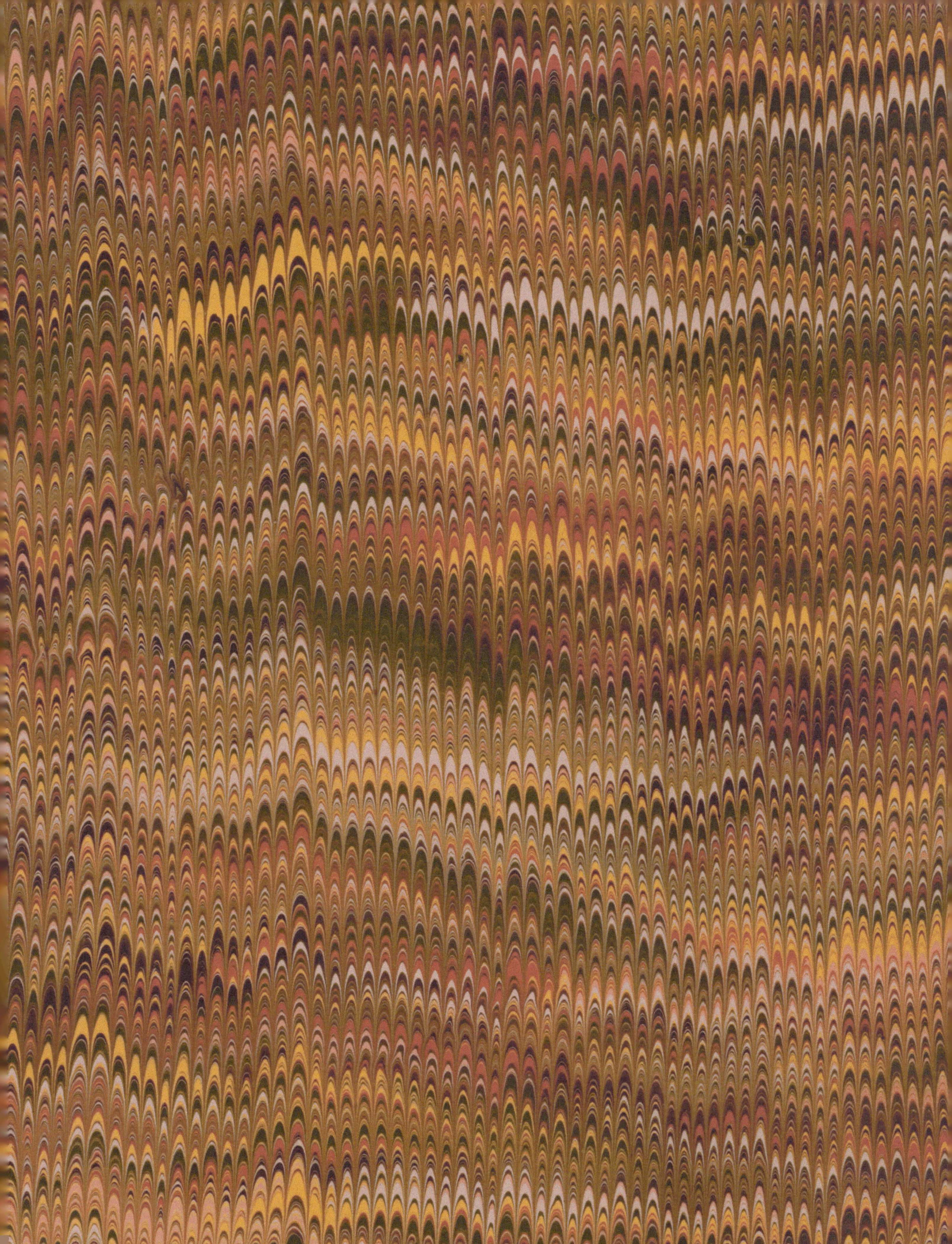

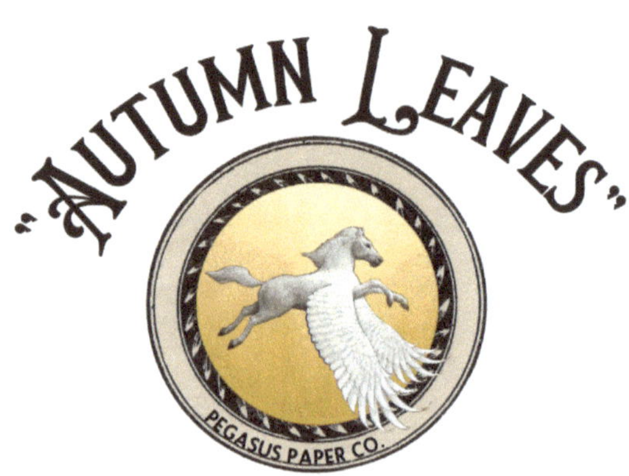

"Autumn Leaves"

Journaling Notepad Insert

A mini project to add into your junk journals, swaps, and Happy mail

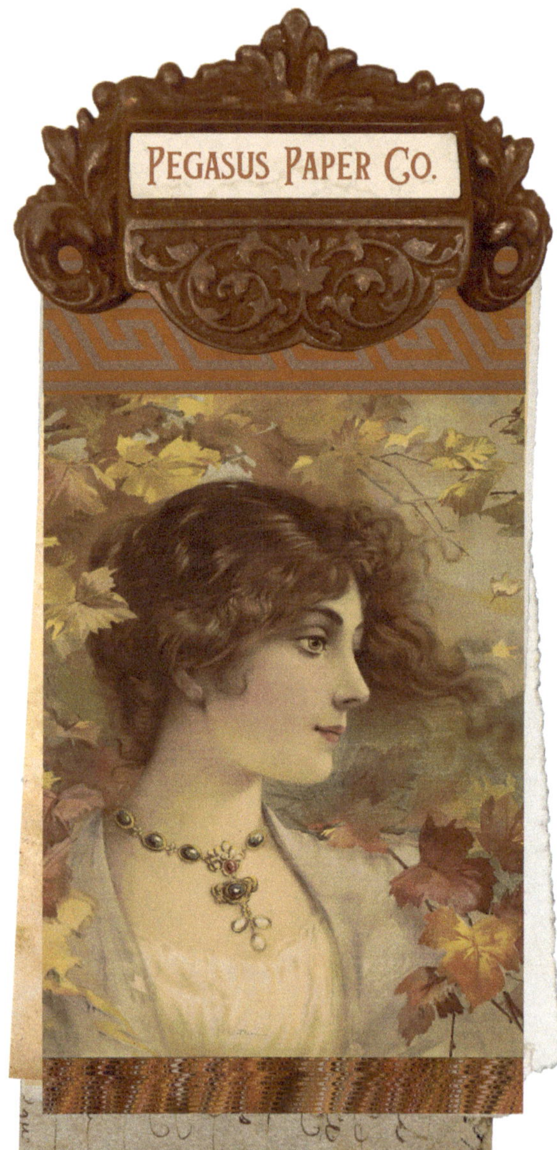

When assembled, it will look like this.

*If you wish to get extra fancy, you can attach ribbons through the circles.

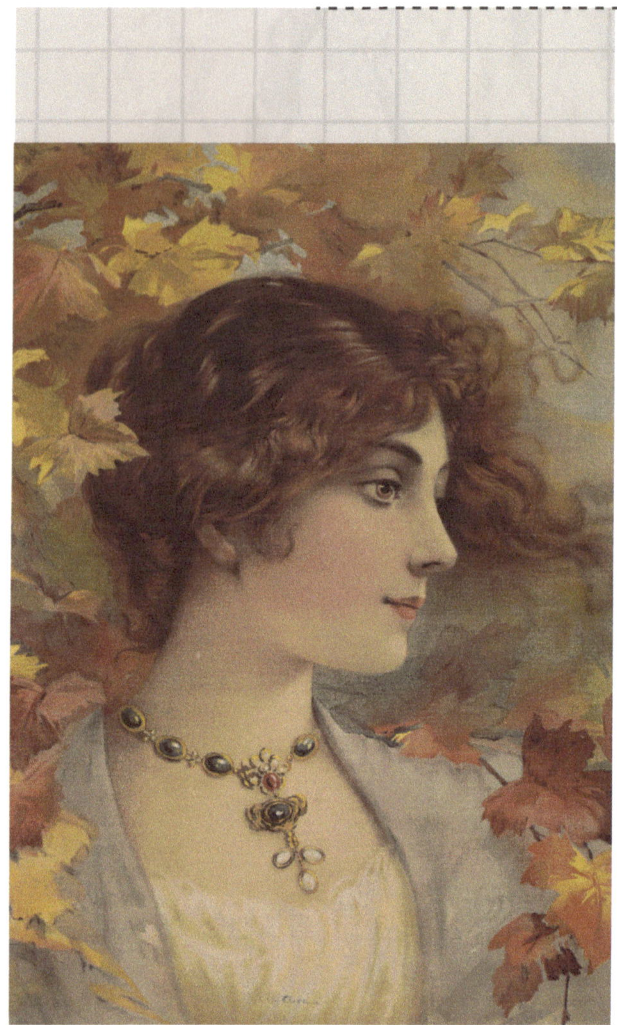

1. Cut out this cover page (with the grid-section, which will be covered in the next step). Then cut the interior pages (on the next page), and put them under this cover page.

2. Fold this paper in half the long way, and staple over the top edge of the gathered papers you want in your notepad

3. Cut out this hardware and glue it to the notepad, then attach the finished set to any page in your journal.

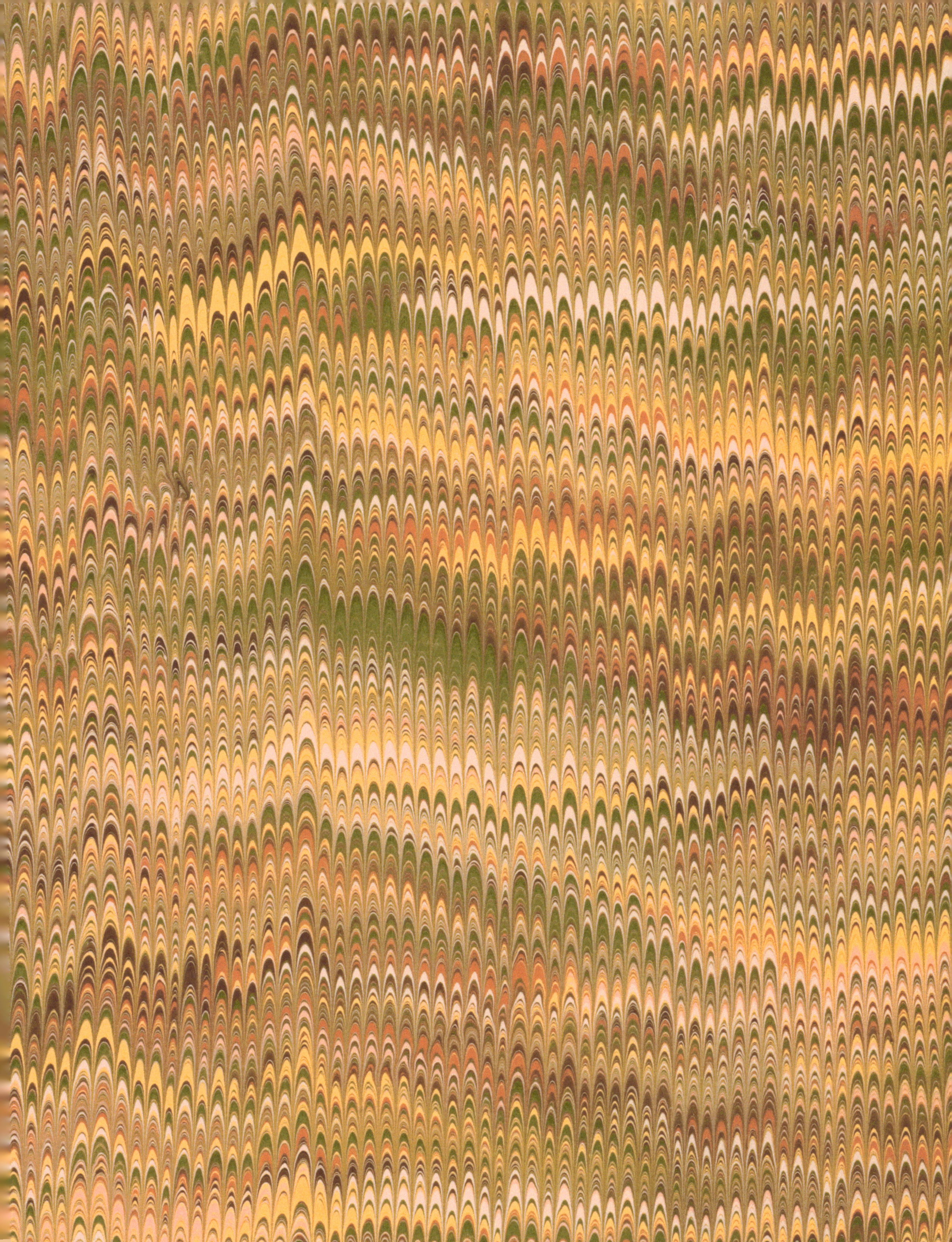

Journaling Notepad Insert – Interior pages

You can use these papers, or choose favorites from your own collection. Tea-stained, printed, blank. Mix and match!

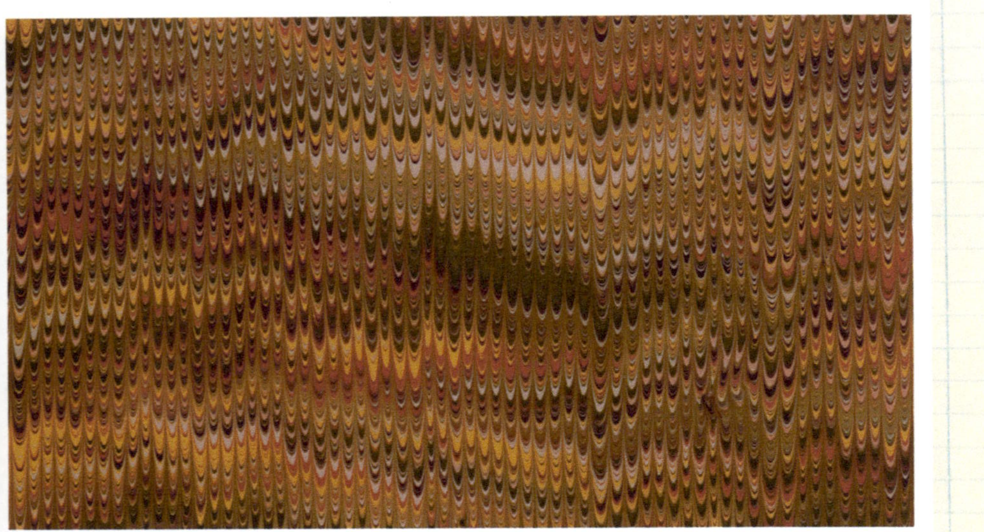

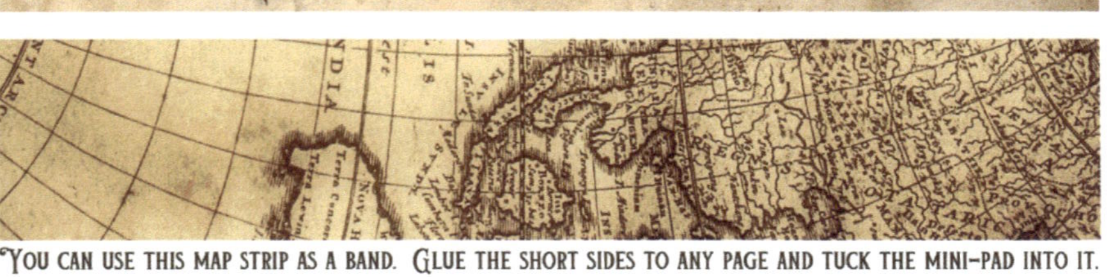

You can use this map strip as a band. Glue the short sides to any page and tuck the mini-pad into it.

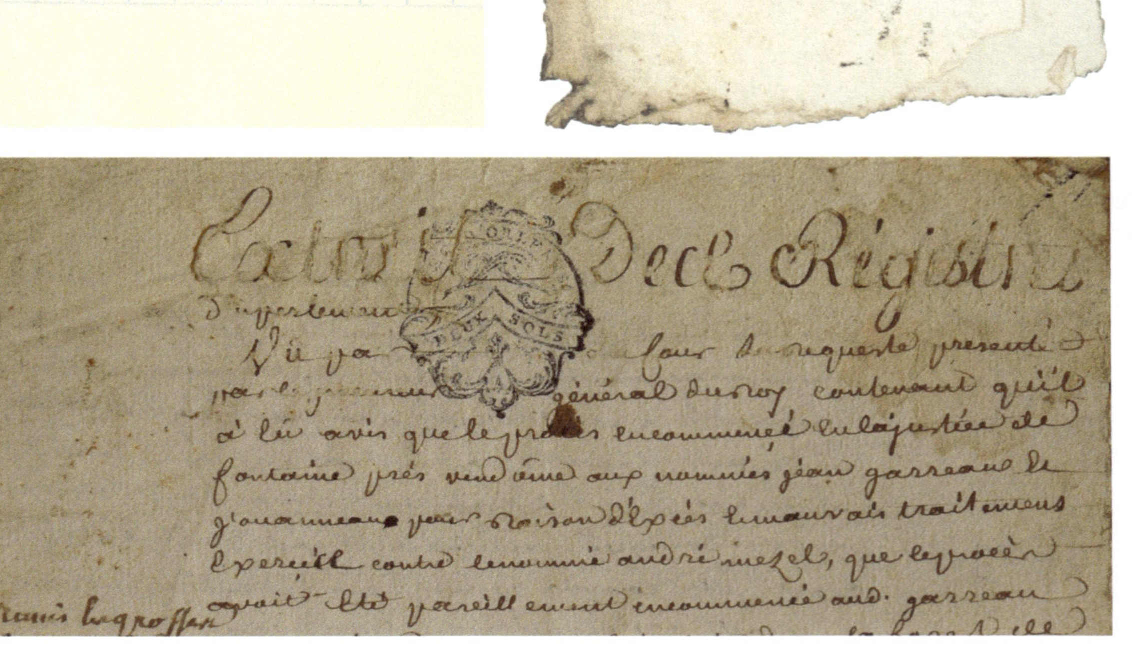

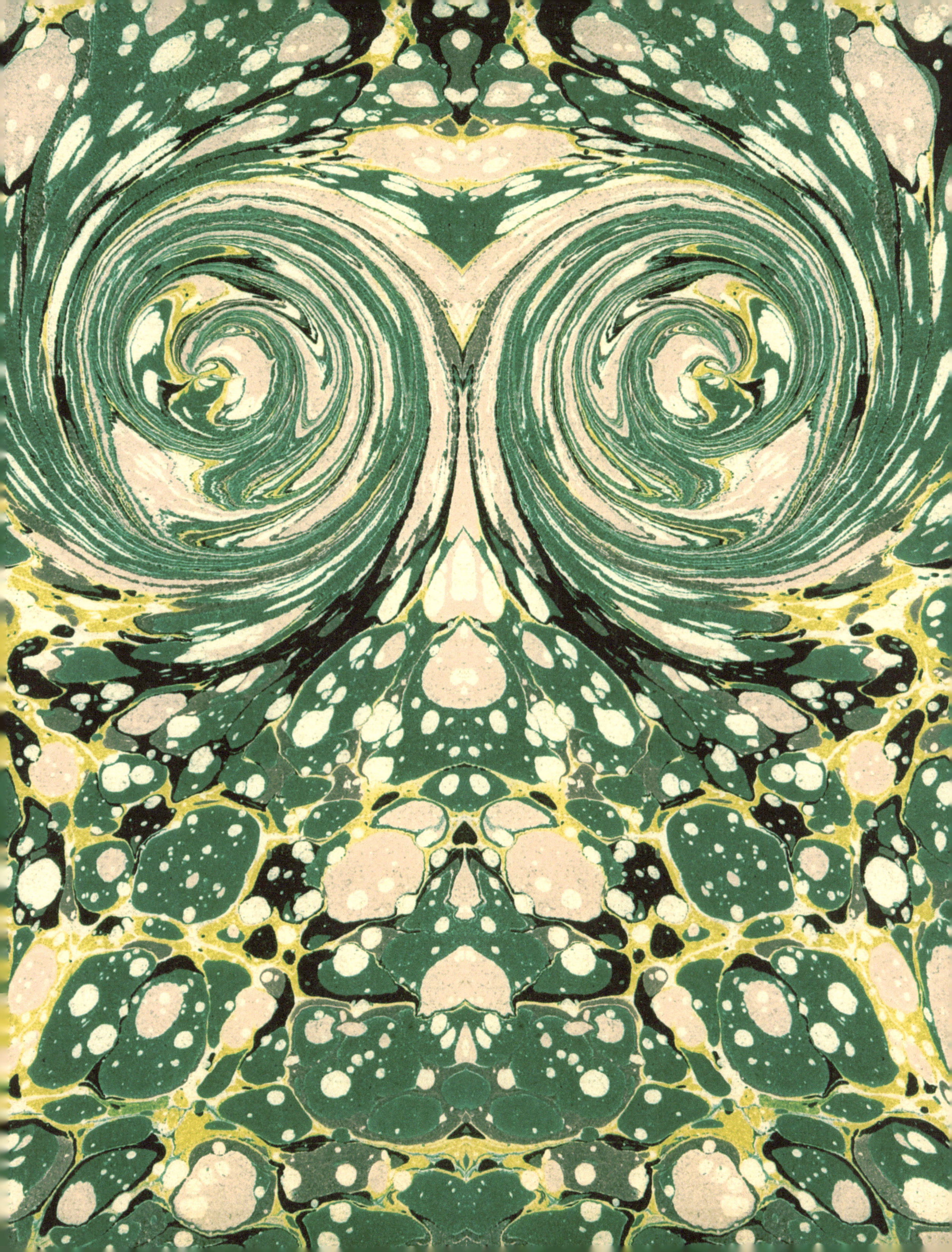

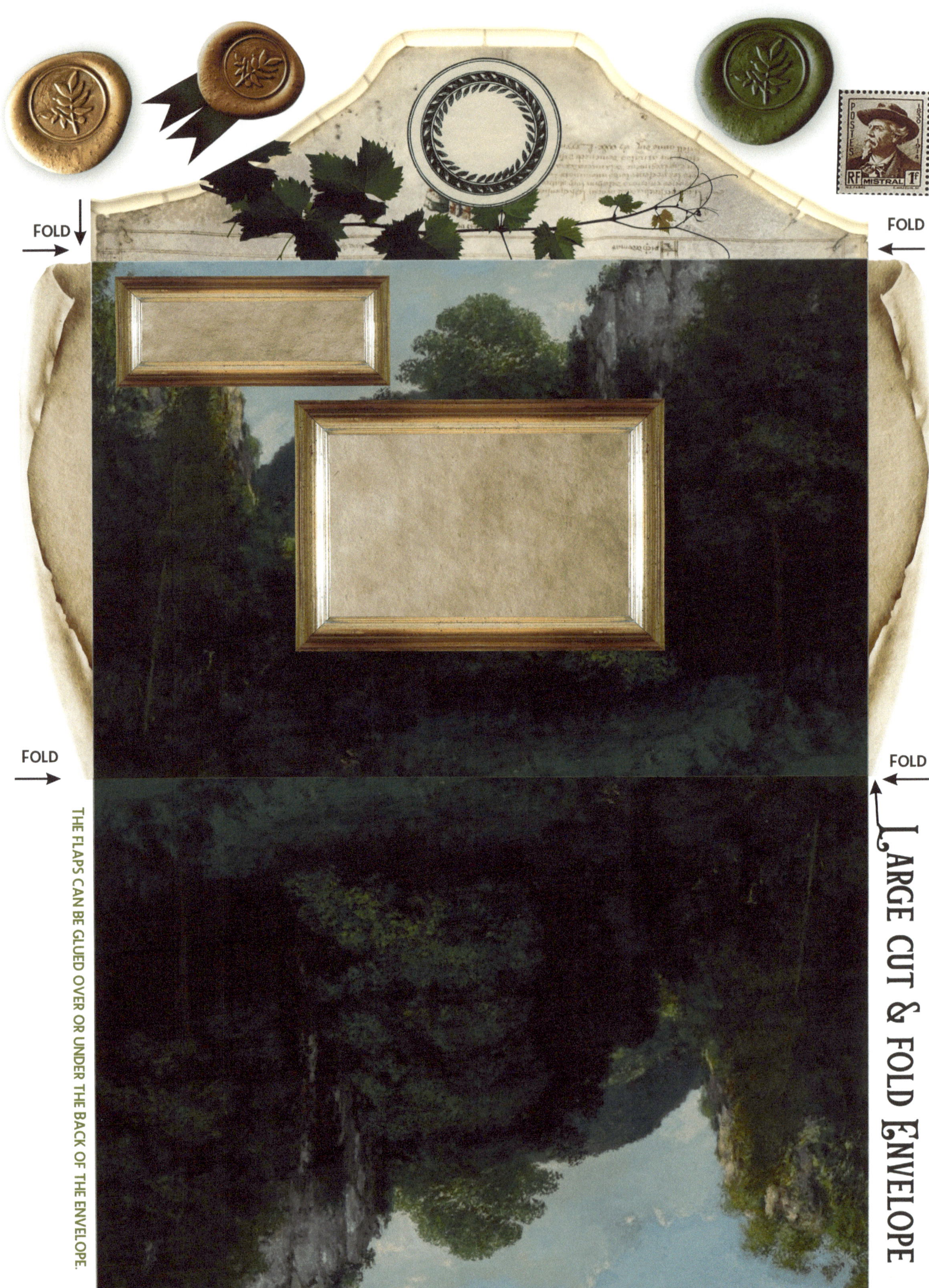

FOLD
FOLD
FOLD
FOLD
POSTES
RF MISTRAL 1f
THE FLAPS CAN BE GLUED OVER OR UNDER THE BACK OF THE ENVELOPE.
LARGE CUT & FOLD ENVELOPE

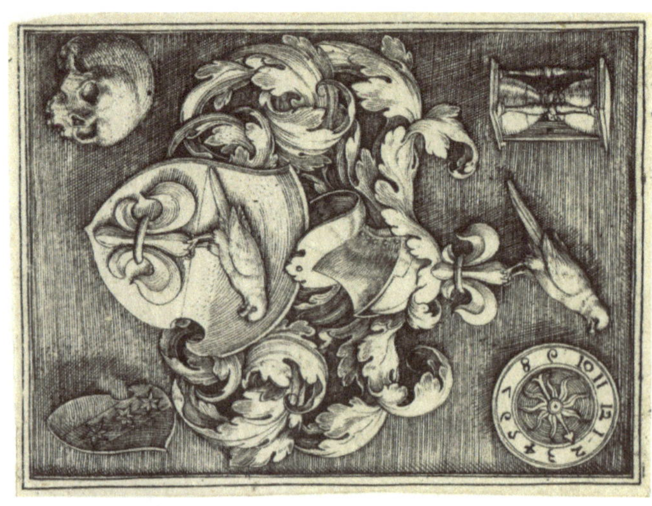

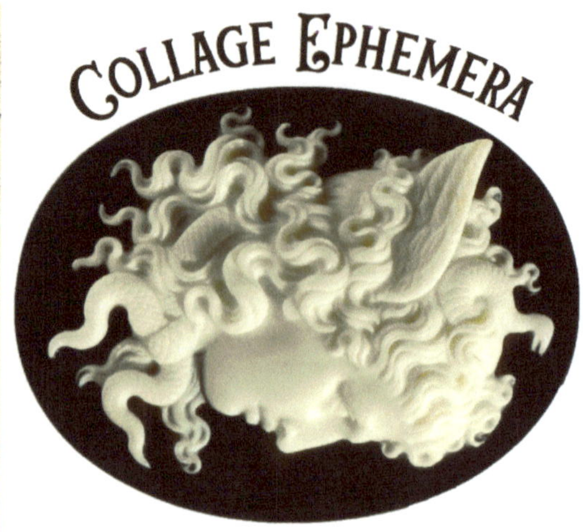

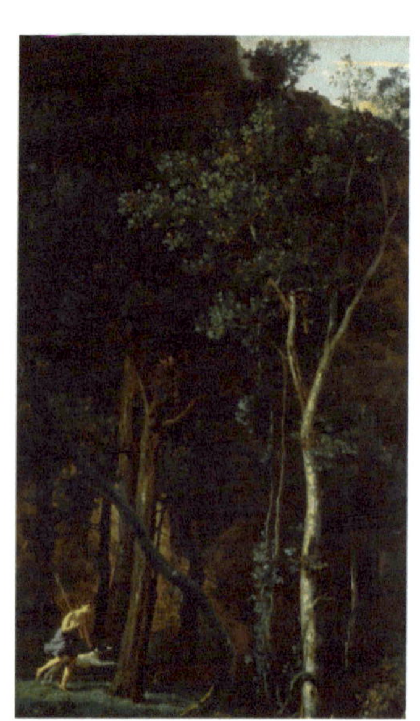

CARD FOR THE LARGE CUT & FOLD ENVELOPE

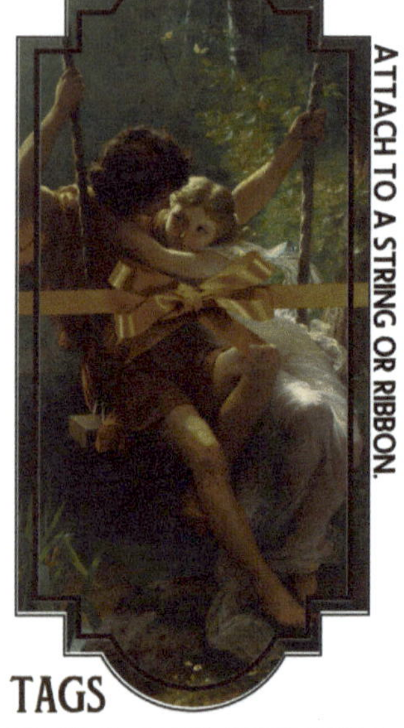

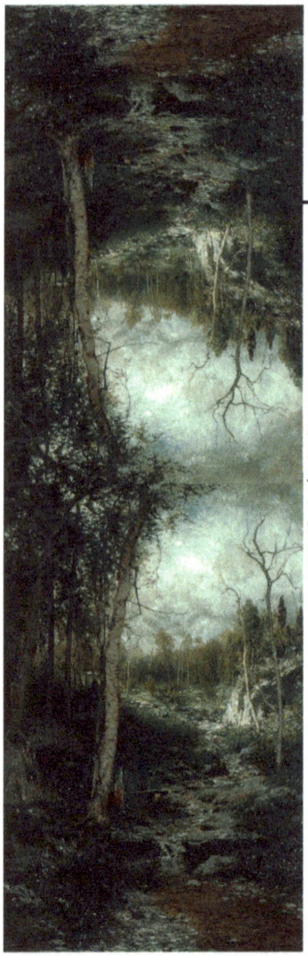

TAGS

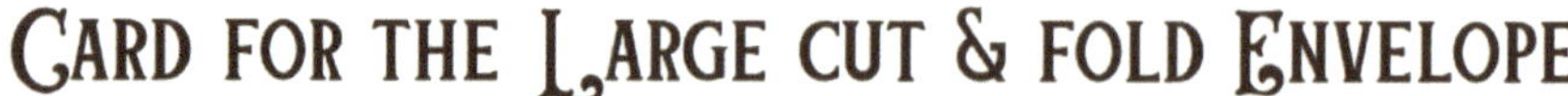

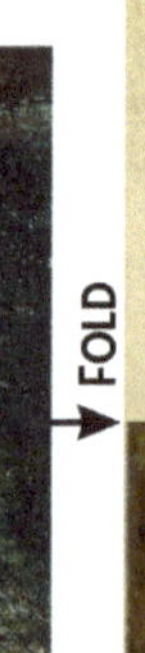

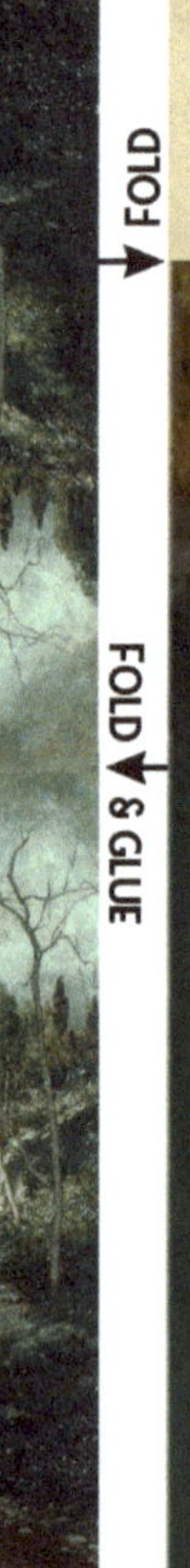

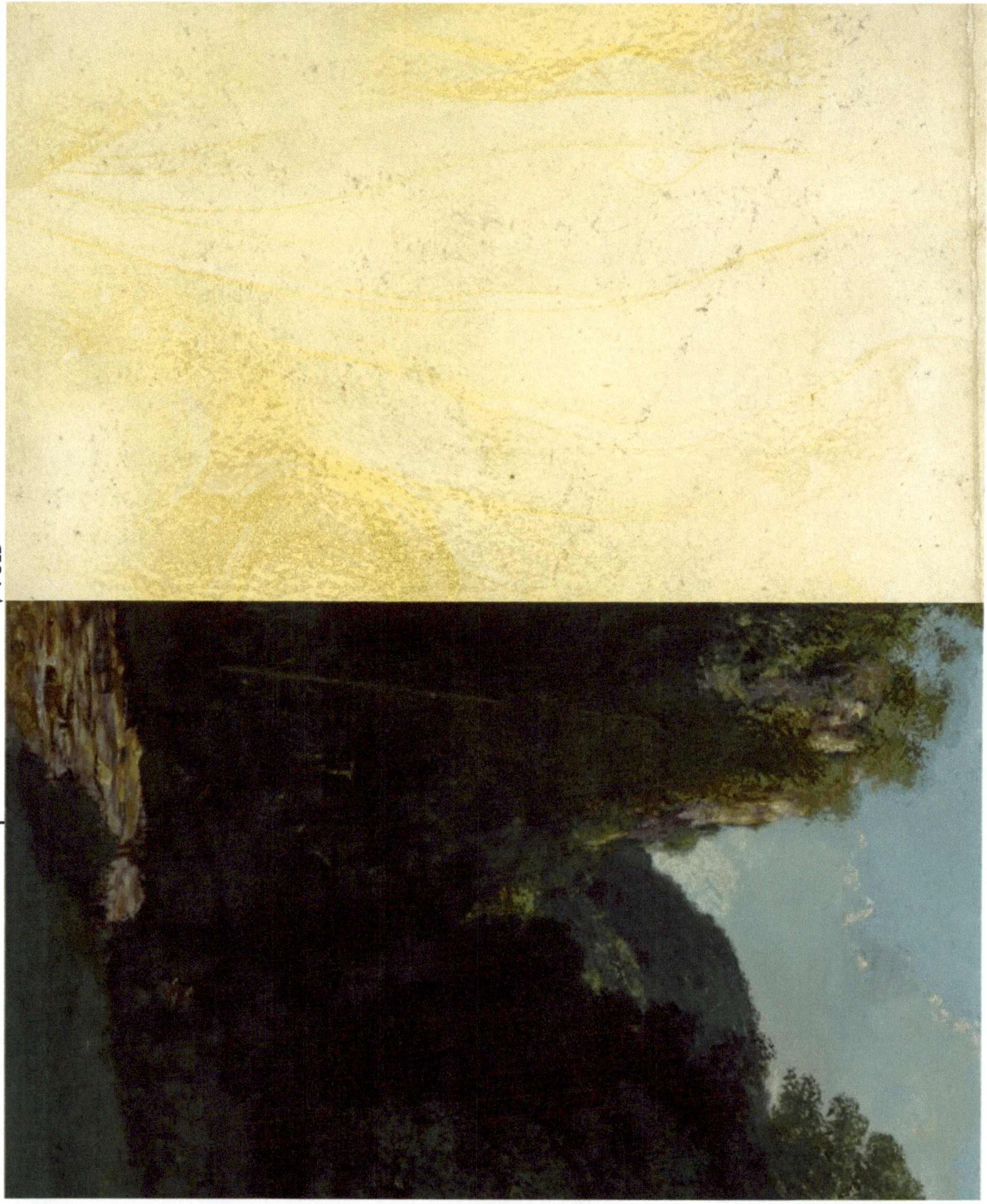

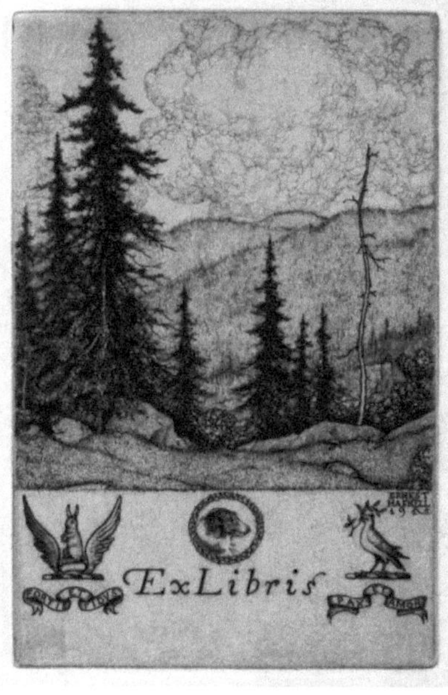

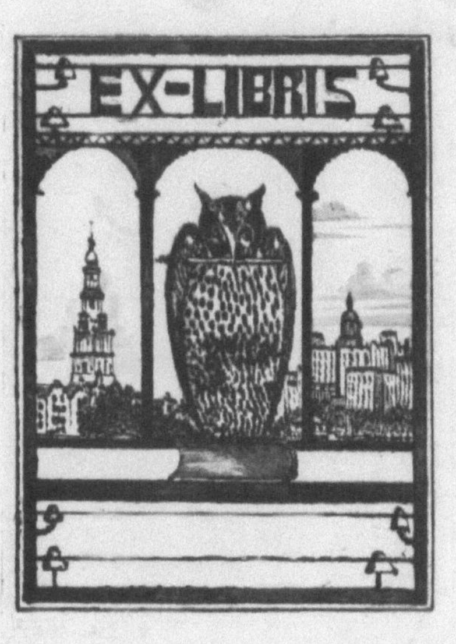

BOOKPLATES

Ex Libris means "from the library of." Write your name in a bookplate and glue it into your journal

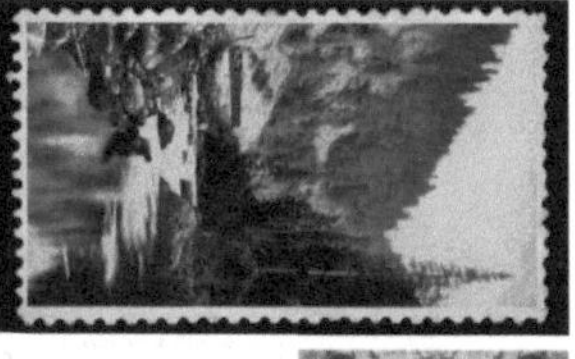

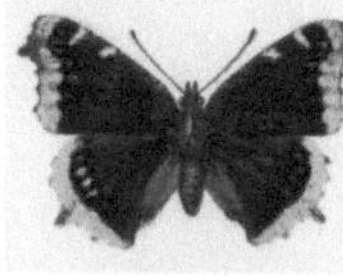

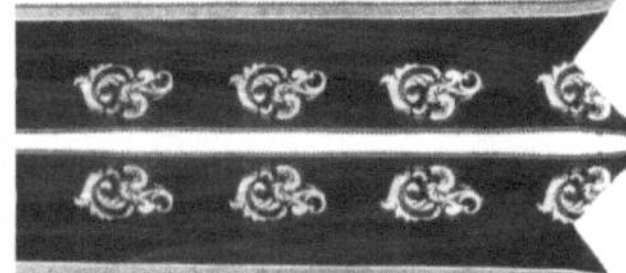

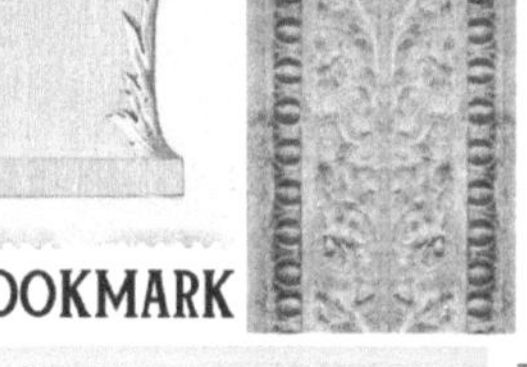

BOOKMARK

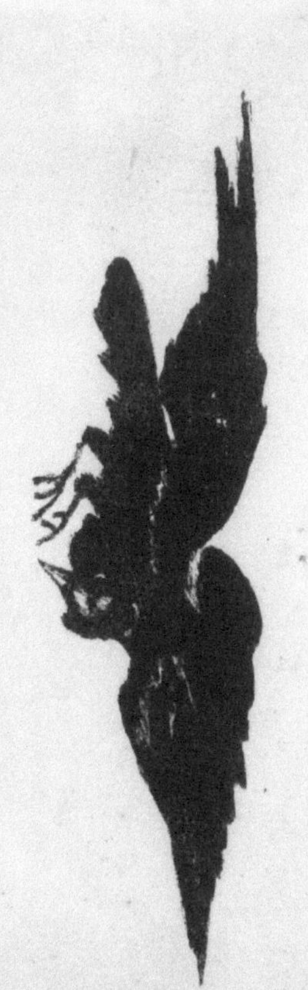

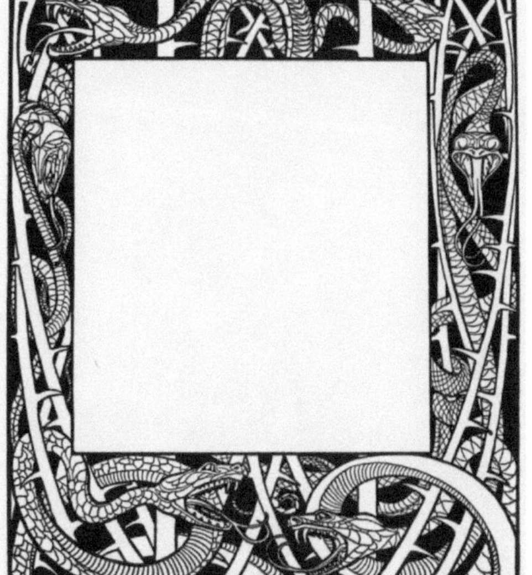

STAMPS & COLLAGE EPHEMERA

These can be used to decorate your journal. You can rub ink on the edges to make them look older. Add tassels and ribbons, tint them with colored pencils... decorate & have fun!

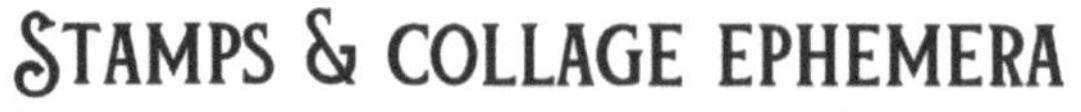

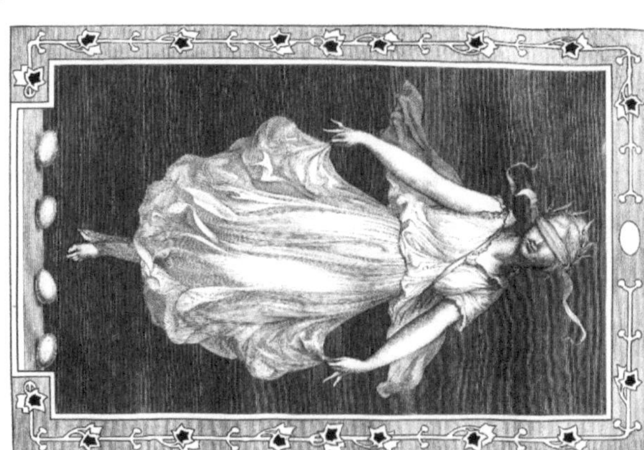

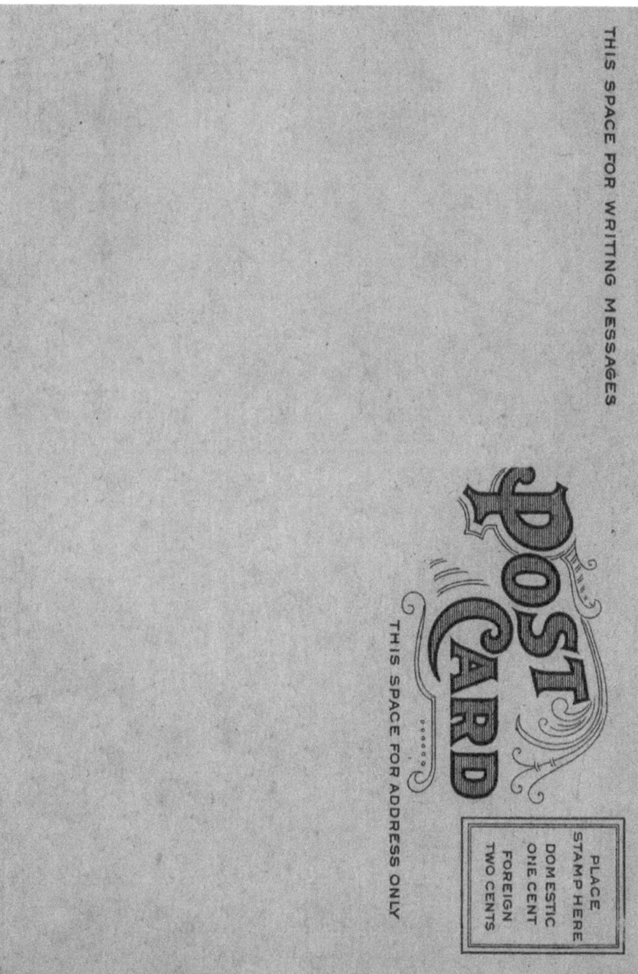

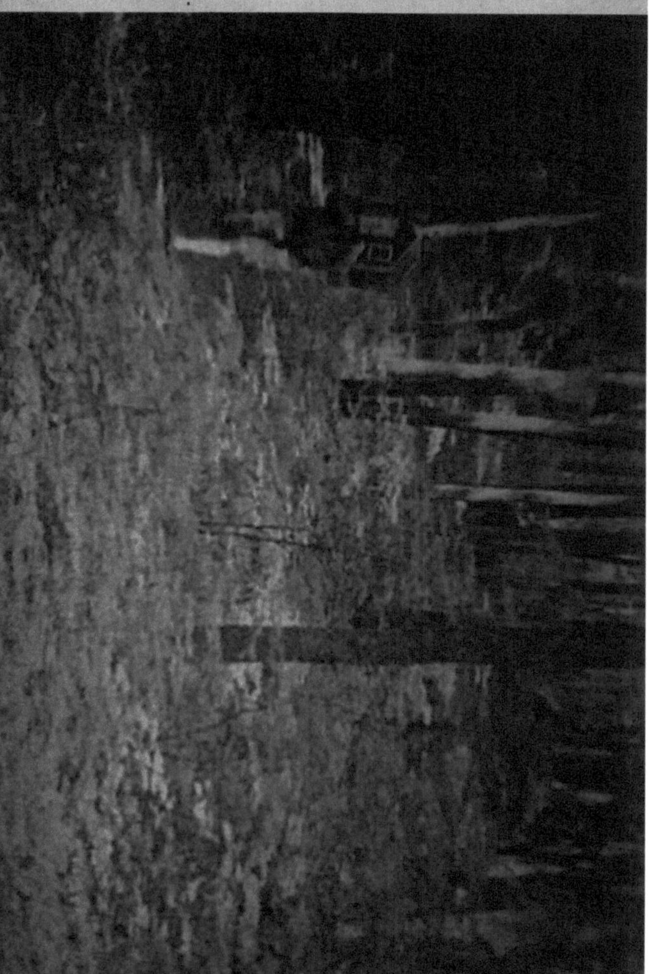

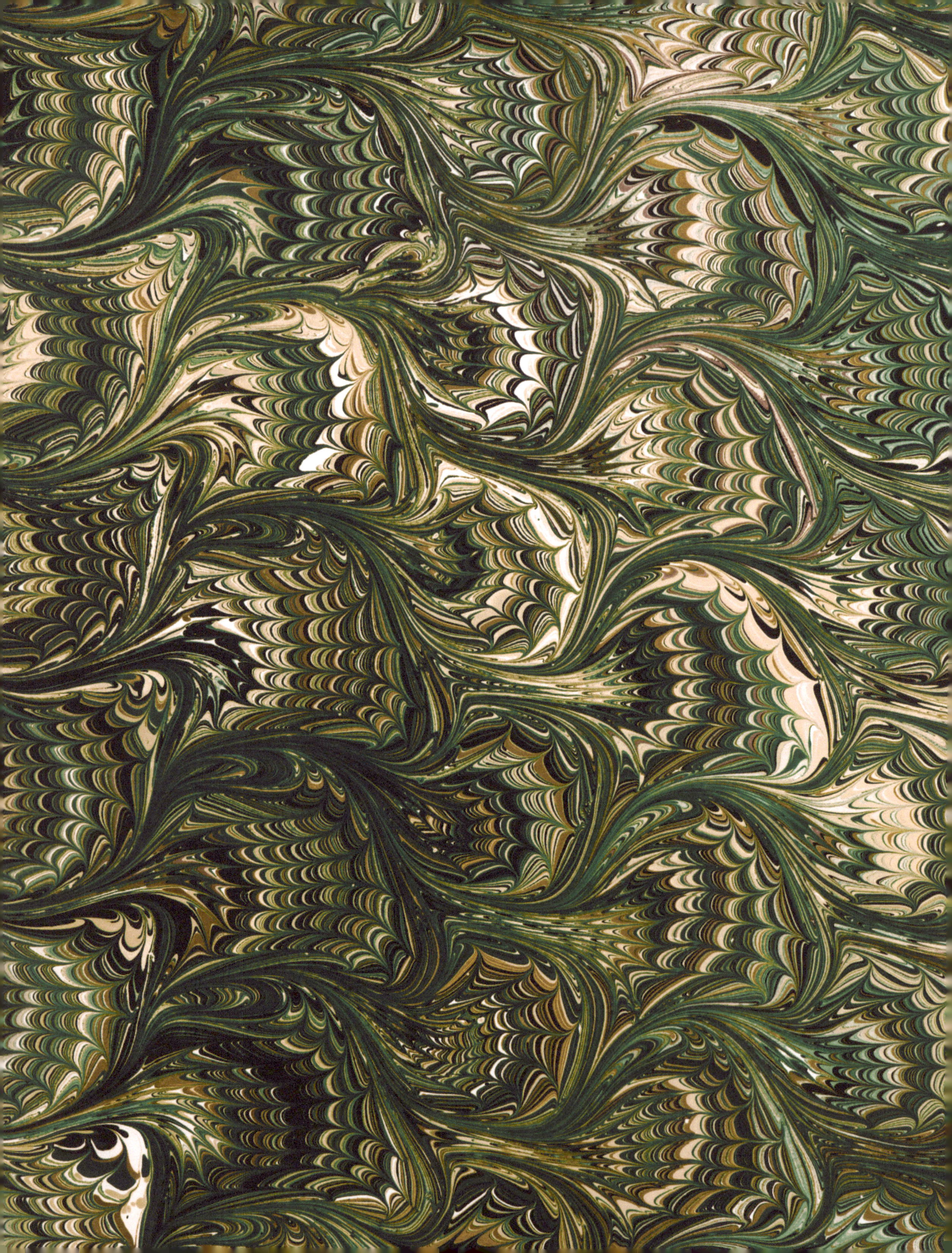

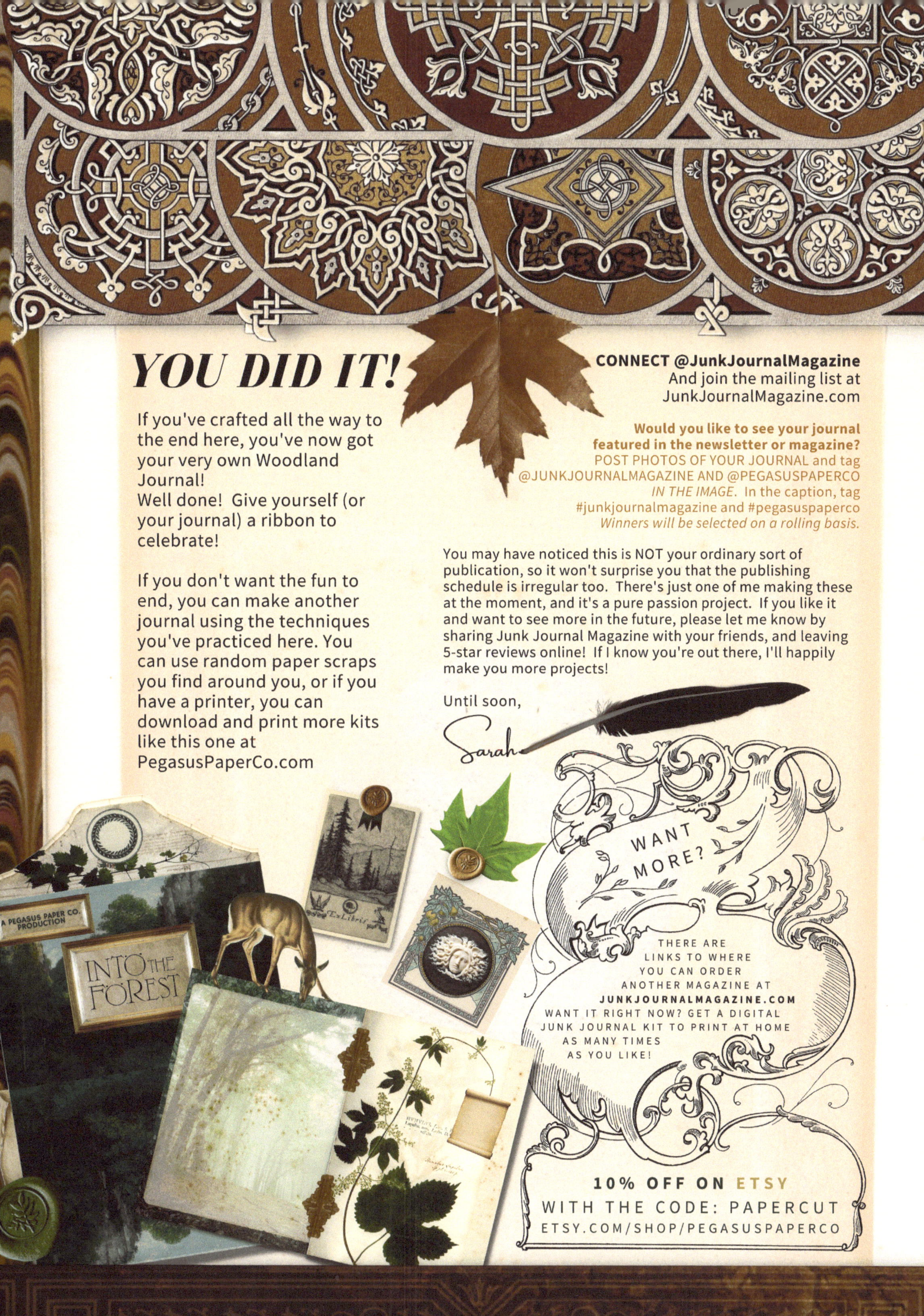

YOU DID IT!

If you've crafted all the way to the end here, you've now got your very own Woodland Journal!
Well done! Give yourself (or your journal) a ribbon to celebrate!

If you don't want the fun to end, you can make another journal using the techniques you've practiced here. You can use random paper scraps you find around you, or if you have a printer, you can download and print more kits like this one at
PegasusPaperCo.com

CONNECT @JunkJournalMagazine
And join the mailing list at
JunkJournalMagazine.com

Would you like to see your journal featured in the newsletter or magazine?
POST PHOTOS OF YOUR JOURNAL and tag @JUNKJOURNALMAGAZINE AND @PEGASUSPAPERCO *IN THE IMAGE.* In the caption, tag #junkjournalmagazine and #pegasuspaperco
Winners will be selected on a rolling basis.

You may have noticed this is NOT your ordinary sort of publication, so it won't surprise you that the publishing schedule is irregular too. There's just one of me making these at the moment, and it's a pure passion project. If you like it and want to see more in the future, please let me know by sharing Junk Journal Magazine with your friends, and leaving 5-star reviews online! If I know you're out there, I'll happily make you more projects!

Until soon,

Sarah